*The*
# MARTIAL ARTS
*of*
# ANCIENT GREECE

# The
# MARTIAL ARTS
## of
# ANCIENT GREECE

*Modern Fighting Techniques
from the Age of Alexander*

KOSTAS DERVENIS
and
NEKTARIOS LYKIARDOPOULOS

Translated by Michael J. Pantelides
and
Kostas Dervenis

Destiny Books
Rochester, Vermont

Destiny Books
One Park Street
Rochester, Vermont 05767
www.DestinyBooks.com

Destiny Books is a division of Inner Traditions International

Originally published in Greek under the title ΠΟΛΕΜΙΚΕΣ ΤΕΧΝΕΣ ΣΤΗΝ
ΑΡΧΑΙΑ ΕΛΛΑΔΑ ΚΑΙ ΤΗ ΜΕΣΟΓΕΙΟ [Martial Arts in Ancient Greece and
the Mediterranean] by Esoptron Publications
First U.S. Edition published in 2007 by Destiny Books

**Library of Congress Cataloging-in-Publication Data**
Dervenis, Kostas.
  The martial arts of ancient Greece : modern fighting techniques from the Age of
Alexander / Kostas Dervenis and Nektarios Lykiardopoulos ; translated by Michael
J. Pantelides and Kostas Dervenis. — 1st U.S. ed.
      p. cm.
  Includes bibliographical references and index.
  ISBN-13: 978-1-59477-192-7 (pbk.)
  ISBN-10: 1-59477-192-8 (pbk.)
  1. Pancratium—Greece—History. 2. Martial arts—Greece—History. I. Lykiardo-
poulos, Nektarios. II. Title.
  GV1193.D47 2007
  796.810938—dc22
                                                                   2007031292

Printed and bound in the United States by PA Hutchinson

10 9 8 7 6 5 4 3 2 1

Text design and layout by Jon Desautels
This book was typeset in Sabon with Schneidler used as a display typeface

# CONTENTS

# PREFACE

A distinction has always existed between combat sports and martial arts—the former being controlled athletic contests, the latter training exercises for actual battle. This demarcation has been recognized as a matter of controversy in the historical record, and beyond that, it would seem that the difference between the two activities reaches far back into the mists of prehistory. Combat sports initially grew out of primal religious festivities, a replication (or evolution) of the duelling of males of all species during the annual spring mating rites. While such contests originated as bloody duels, people soon realized that killing or maiming their own warriors to determine suitable breeding stock was not in a society's best interest. So rules were developed to prevent permanent injury or death and combat sports were differentiated from actual battle, in which, sadly, there are no rules and never have been.

Also a matter of controversy is the very important question of whether the practice of combat sports (and martial arts) leads to positive or negative psychological changes in the participants. There are many today who claim that practicing the martial arts and combat sports develops beneficial psychological changes and encourages correct societal integration; however, most of the positive benefits determined by the related studies have to do with modern combat sports of an Eastern origin. In contrast, other researchers claim that participating in socially sanctioned combative sports encourages violence and aggression. Certainly the popularity of pay-for-view, no-holds-barred "mixed martial arts" tournaments provides the general public with a view of combat sports that tends to remind one of a Roman arena. While combat sports did indeed grow out of actual battle tactics designed for conditions under which one must kill or be killed, throughout history they have evolved to address more diverse goals, such as personal growth and self-discipline. Sadly, in today's age of crass commercialism, pay-for-view combat sports have come to emulate the decadence of the Roman arena, with amateur activities being relegated to a lesser level of importance in the mind of the public.

In ancient Greece, the sport of pankration arose as an attempt to introduce martial arts competition into the ancient Greek Olympiad. *Pankration* is an ancient Greek word that means "total control/power" and refers to a combat sport that was essentially an all-out fight between two contestants. Pankration allowed bare-knuckle boxing, kicking, wrestling, jointlocks, throws, and strangleholds, prohibiting only two tactics: biting and gouging out the opponent's eyes. (There were other prohibitions, but only the two aforementioned were "written in stone"; the rest were up to the judges.) Pankration contests were held in stadiums and it was indeed a spectator sport. The emphasis, however, was clearly on skill and not on blood; in fact, the contest had to be "bloodless" *(anaimaktos)*. The ancient Greeks were preoccupied with the notion of an "honorable struggle" *(eugeni amilla)* during athletic competition.

The emphasis in combative sports was on "control," not on brutality. This precept is clearly established by the word *pankration* itself. The term does not mean "all powers," as it has been erroneously translated in the past. In fact, the word *kratos* is used in modern Greek and means "nation." While no exact translation for the word *kratos* is possible in English, and while "power" is very much a part of the meaning of the term *pankration,* it is obvious that "control" should be considered in equal proportion, since it is not in the interest of a "nation" to exterminate or hospitalize its citizens. Hence, pankration should be thought of as "submission fighting," with the concept of *eugeni amilla* (honorable struggle) liberally applied. The athletes did not seek to hurt their opponents, but rather to subdue them through skillful means.* In this

---

*This characteristic of the term *pankration* was first published internationally by the authors (in Greek) in 2002. The use of the term *pammachon* in reference to Greek martial arts was established earlier by Kostas Dervenis in 2000. This intellectual property right has been abused by other authors since then, without permission, authorization, or reference.

context, both training for pankration and practice of the sport provided a useful educational medium for ancient society. In modern times, Dr. Jigoro Kano established a similar conduit for his ancestral martial arts through the establishment of judo as an international combat sport.

In the past few decades there has been renewed interest in, and considerable literary effort dedicated to, pankration. In addition, quite a few modern martial artists of Greek descent have pictured themselves as the regenerators of the sport, creating modern synthesis systems, which are usually a combination of kickboxing, sport judo, and sport wrestling. This book will attempt to analyze both the kinesiology and techniques of the ancient Greek combat sport, and show its relationship to—and differences from—Greek martial arts, where appropriate. We will also try to answer, in a historical context, the question of whether practicing combat sports (and martial arts) can lead to positive or negative psychological changes in the participants.

We will attempt to address these questions, not for love of the past, but for hope in the future. Many of the aforementioned Greek martial artists of today, hoping to restore pankration to a preeminent position in the world of combat sports, are sadly missing the point in their pursuit of material gain.* In today's world, it matters little whether or not "the Greeks were the first to use a shoulder throw" (they were not) or "Alexander the Great brought pankration to the warriors of India" (chances are he did not). What matters are the problems we face globally as a species: accelerating industrialization, rapid population growth, widespread malnutrition, depletion of nonrenewable resources, and a deteriorating environment. If these problems are not dealt with, the most probable result will be a rather sudden and uncontrollable decline in population within the next one hundred years—this is a clinical way of saying that billions of people will die. That having been said, experts agree that it is possible, even now, to alter these growth trends and to establish a condition of ecological and economic stability that would be sustainable far into the future. This state of global equilibrium could be designed so that the basic material needs of each person on Earth are satisfied and each person has an equal opportunity to realize his individual human potential.

---

*Neither of the authors are professional instructors of the martial arts or combat sports; instead, they are motivated by an amateur's love of these activities.

We believe that both combat sports and the martial arts can play a role in this hopeful future by being be used as a training tool to facilitate such equilibrium within the individual. Because any mass societal action begins at the level of the citizen, and because an individual trained in the classical ideals of combat sports or the martial arts is more likely to exhibit self-restraint and societal altruism, we are convinced that such training will replicate itself fractally in societies and nations as a whole, and play a part in saving our planet. We believe that a study of the martial arts and combat sports of the ancient Mediterranean may contribute to this salvation, if for no other reason than that they played a crucial part in the development of classical Western civilization as a whole.

For those readers less interested in global ideals and goals, this book represents the first thorough technical analysis of the ancient martial arts of the Mediterranean, as interpreted in the light of modern martial techniques. But it is here that we must offer a word of caution to athletes and martial artists who will in turn (given the tendencies of the Internet) try to use our words as gospel: this book is only our opinion. While it is true that the human body moves only in certain ways, and that we are convinced that specific techniques have remained unchanged around the world for thousands of millennia, we did indeed base this research on our knowledge of modern techniques. Often, in looking for the trees, we miss the forest—people should be very careful in what they claim. We ourselves have tried to be careful; we ask that others be equally careful when using our words.

We must close this preface with a case in point regarding the above caution. In the past year, we have been exposed to attempts by popular media to identify modern mixed martial arts with classical pankration. There are political reasons for making this identification, which the authors oppose, and while we will not get into them here, we do wish to note that we consider such attempts as theft of Greek culture, identity, and history. And, historically speaking, the perpetrators are considerably off base; they are like scientists who attempt to "doctor" an experiment's results to reach the conclusion they desire, rather than the conclusions that nature would give them on her own.

We can offer a good example of this: both authors have been personally exposed to actual traditions of Greek martial arts and combat sports. Nektarios's grandfather was a championship wrestler in Athens during the early twentieth century; Kostas is from a village where the last vestiges of a nineteenth-century combative art survived until the Second World War. One must be careful when using the word *traditional*. The term does not refer to a "museum practice" or to a reenactment, and the authors are not suggesting that we have inherited the battle tactics of the ancient *hoplite* warriors. In fact, the word *tradition* means that knowledge and practices are "traded" from generation to generation, and hence become the property of each specific generation in turn. Greek folk songs were played on a reed instrument called a *zournas* in the nineteenth century—today they are played on clarinets. Techniques and practices are often modified and adapted by the current "owners" as they deem fit; in regards to a surviving martial tradition, they must be tailored to fit the weapons and tactics of the day and age, otherwise the tradition dies out. Certainly this is the case for Greek martial arts, which did not survive, generally speaking, even in Greece itself. In the photos shown here, we would like to provide clear documentary evidence, for the first time in the West, of the existence of nineteenth-century Greek martial arts. These arts were practiced in northern Greece throughout the nineteenth and early twentieth centuries. The photo of staff training was taken around 1890. The photo of unarmed combat training was taken in 1905.* These martial traditions most likely may be traced back to the fourteenth century CE, and will be the subject of a further volume. In the context of *this* book, we refer to the existence of these traditional martial arts for a specific reason: as can be clearly seen by any experienced hoplologist, the techniques exhibited have nothing to do with Mixed Martial Arts, and look more Eastern than Western (in fact, the movements have to do with the use of weapons).

Figure P.1. Students in northern Greece practicing martial arts staff training around 1890.

Figure P.2. Northern Greek students practicing unarmed combat training in 1905.

If such errors in the interpretation of martial tradition can be made within an individual's lifetime (Kostas's grandfather was taught this martial art in Elementary school), how many errors can be made in compilation and analysis of technique over the centuries? Thousands? Tens of thousands? Clearly one should be very careful in making historical claims, or in referring to, modern mixed martial arts as pankration—there are considerable, and very real, differences in technique, principles, and reasons for practicing the respective sports. These are evident to those who have actually taken the time and trouble to investigate them. We offer this book as our best attempt to set the record straight.

---

*These photos may not be used without the expressed consent of the authors.

# 1

# THE BIRTH OF PAMMACHON

War is interwoven with the history of humanity. From our earliest days in school, we are taught about the victories of diverse conquerors throughout the ages, and of the empires they forged that marked the development of humankind. Despite appearances, however, human beings were not always warlike and aggressive. The bands of people that roamed the earth twelve thousand years ago, for example, were for the most part peaceful, living off the abundant game and gathering fruits, bulbs, and tubers where they found them. We know today that people *did* fight among themselves even then, but as their way of life was unfettered by the concept of ownership, war was an exception, not the rule. Perhaps the Norwegian explorer Fridtjof Nansen was the last of modern men to catch a glimpse of this fading world, as the first European to come into contact with the Eskimos living on the Greenland icecap in 1888. These Eskimos still lived off nature's bounty at the time, just as their ancestors had for millennia. Nansen wrote:

> Fighting and brutalities of that sort . . . are unknown to them, and murder is very rare. They hold it atrocious to kill a fellow creature; therefore war in their eyes is incomprehensible and repulsive, a thing for which their language has no word; soldiers and officers, brought up in the trade of killing, they regard as mere butchers.*

---

*Time-Life Books, *The Enterprise of War* (Amsterdam: Time-Life Books, 1991).

1

# BLADED WEAPONS AND THE
# MARTIAL ARTS THROUGHOUT HISTORY

Archaeological data indicates that organized warfare has its roots in Mesopotamia. Of course, things are not as simple as this statement would have us believe; people have been fighting and killing each other for at least forty thousand years, more often than not over food. In fact, quite a few exhumed Stone Age graves have revealed skeletons with flint blades lodged in their rib cages. There is even the possibility (which many of us hope is remote) that Neanderthal man was subjected to genocide by his Cro-Magnon brethren. For all that, it is safe to say that war as an institution did not exist before the breakthrough of agriculture, for the simple reason that before we began farming, we really had no concept of property. With the establishment of agriculture, we "fell from Paradise," and, to further quote the Bible, "saw that we were naked."

In Mesopotamia, then, around the tenth millennium BCE, people systemized cultivation for the first time. This new way of life spread quickly from East to West, establishing a new dynamic in human relations, that of the ownership of land. Those who possessed land to cultivate wanted to keep it; those who didn't, desired it; while still others who did own land but were possessed of greed, wanted more.

It is no coincidence then that around this time we also see spectacular developments in weapons technology. For more than seventy thousand years the main weapons used by men in the hunt were the spear and the javelin. The first "blades" were sharpened stones or pieces of bone or antler. The next step was to place these "blades" on a wooden staff to keep prey or predators at bay during the kill. Our ancestors had learned to do this with fire-hardened sharpened sticks earlier; attaching the "blade" was a logical step. In the process, the true spear and the true ax—weapons that could penetrate the toughest hide or shatter the limbs of prey and predators—were developed. Still, the hunters of this age normally threw large stones at their prey, and used their spears or axes to finish off their quarry up close. Some bright fellow, through necessity or innovation, eventually came up with the concept of hurling his spear to slay his prey from a distance; hence the javelin was born, with all its subsequent upgrades.

For tens of thousands of years, then, men hunted and fought with spear and javelin. Prey was first struck from a distance; evolution and common sense taught our ancestors that it was safer and easier this way.

In the initial confrontations between men, the same rule was followed: wound the opponent from far away, finish him off with spears and axes up close. In roughly the tenth millennium BCE, two powerful new weapons appeared along with agriculture: the bow and the sling. The range of the primitive bow was about 330 feet, twice as far as that of the javelin. An equally frightful weapon was the sling, which was able to throw sharp stones with great accuracy the same distance, or even further as skill developed. For the following eight millennia, the bow and sling were the primary weapons of war.

As these new inventions more than doubled the range and impact power of projectile weapons, they drastically increased the need for protection. We know that protective measures against long-range weapons became crucial for agricultural societies because city walls were one of the first defensive measures devised against invaders. Jericho, for example (built around 8000 BCE), had walls about ten feet thick and thirteen feet high. The mud-brick houses of Çatal Hüyük in central Anatolia (a middle-Neolithic site) form one continuous wall, and were built without windows or doors (residents entered through a hatch in the roof). Neolithic sites such as these bear testimony to the deadliness of projectile weapons.

Within the parameters of these walls and long-range weapons, another type of weapon slowly made its appearance, the reflection of a different type of philosophy. The sharpened stone, known to humanity from the earliest Paleolithic age, had first been used to skin, scrape, and process game. With the institution of breeding livestock, however, the need for a tool to slaughter animals, and to process their meat and skin, became readily apparent. This need was met by the stone knife *with a handle*.

Because this weapon/tool was closely identified with the taking of life and the growing ritual involved with this action, its use was extended to the assassination of an enemy already injured by projectile weapons. Agricultural societies were by definition initially defensive, since they tended to stay in one place. Hence, wounded enemies were hunted down and executed after a battle (to prevent them from regrouping and attacking again), much like archers will track a wounded deer today. No animal dies willingly, and human beings are no exception; during these assassinations, personal combat was often a necessity. Most likely then, wounded enemies were slaughtered by groups of men, who once again attacked first from a distance, and then up close.

From the sixth millennium BCE, however, comes the first confirmation of a change in ethics, again from the site of Çatal Hüyük. Excavations have uncovered a series of daggers made from flint—their blades are broad, pressure-flaked on one side and ground on the other, while the handles are made of bone. One example among them is exquisite, with the handle winding down in the form of a snake (figure 1.1). This is no butcher's knife, but the ornate and prized possession of a warrior. It was designed for the thrust, and, as such, uniquely fabricated for the personal combat of man against man. It is also obvious that this is a warrior's blade because it is designed for stabbing, and not for cutting. The method used to slaughter animals in the sixth millennium BCE is the same used today: the arteries in the neck are cut and the animal is allowed to bleed to death. In contrast, the most successful way to eliminate an enemy on the battlefield was, and is, to stab him in a vital area. This sort of *grand-guignol* logic has convinced many *hoplologists* (those who study weapons) that the "dagger of Çatal Hüyük" was the weapon of a warrior, used in hand-to-hand combat, and not the ritualistic tool of a butcher or primitive priest.

Weapons like this dagger are not easy to manufacture. They require time, effort, and know-how, and we have turned up no earlier blades so evidently designed with balance, form, and function clearly in mind. *This blade was created by a man who knew how to fight with a knife.* Now, in the early days of organized agriculture, all men were hunters, farmers, and warriors; circumstance and necessity dictated action on an individual basis. But as weapons of destruction became more and more powerful and focused, the need for specialized ability and particular skills developed accordingly. The men who were more inclined and able to use weapons were the ones for whom they were fabricated. And so a warrior class began to take form, though it would not appear in full bloom until the Bronze Age.

We believe that people back then were less twisted than they are now (civilization always has a way of making things both better and worse). The desires and intentions of people, good and bad, were more out in the open. The dagger of Çatal Hüyük cries out its story to us: these men—who were not the animals we have come to see them as—realized that the bloodshed they were causing was a terrible thing. Perhaps their shamans had been warned of the consequences through spirit mediums. So they tried to keep the fighting among themselves: a warrior fought

Figure 1.1. Knife made of flint with bone handle. Çatal Hüyük, Central Turkey, sixth millennium BCE, Ankara Museum. (Drawing based on museum photograph.)

only a warrior, and they fought by mutual consent. Certainly there was a large portion of ego involved as well ("I will fight only those who are worthy of me").

But the dagger we are discussing is not a butcher's tool, and there are other weapons that lend themselves better to simple execution. A spear, for example, is much safer than a dagger. Even a stout club or ax is better, and less costly to make. This dagger is a warrior's back-up weapon, something that he used in battle "up close and personal," a weapon that lent itself for use in a duel. In short, *these men wanted to give their enemy a fighting chance*—and thus the duel was born along with the warrior class.

The second weapon of this kind that has turned up as archaeological evidence comes from Egypt, and dates from the fourth millennium BCE (figure 1.2). This knife, whose blade is also made of flint, has been clearly designed for slashing and cutting, not for stabbing. Nevertheless, its handle is decorated with carved images of warriors in hand-to-hand combat. We therefore believe that this knife also belonged to a warrior, though some will argue that its use was ritual slaughter due to the shape of the blade. (Suffice it to say that the "cut vs. thrust" argument in knife dueling still goes on today.)

It is safe to say, then, that the warrior class has been in existence since the sixth millennium BCE. Such men assumed, for the most part, the burden of war. Perhaps the existence of the Çatal Hüyük dagger also specifies the millennium during which the martial arts took shape. Beyond our personal love and knowledge of the combative arts, submission wrestling, and history, we base this conclusion on the Greek language itself. The words *máche* (meaning "battle" or "combat") and *máchaera* (meaning "knife") both stem from the same root, *mach* (μάχ), in ancient Greek—a poetically exact and particularly mathematical tongue. We believe that this is not coincidental: máche and máchaera are defined within the same context, a battle to the death between warriors using close-quarter combat weaponry—a knife, hatchet, sword, or spear. Consequently, these two words also define the development of the martial or combative arts—referred to here with the archaic word *pammachon* (a compound word formed from *pan* meaning "all" plus máche)—which are the product of hand-to-hand combat involving bladed weapons.

Incidentally, it is possible to make an interesting study of the martial arts simply by examining the play of words used to describe them.

Figure 1.2. Knife made of flint with ivory handle from Gebel el-Arak. The relief on the handle depicts hand-to-hand combat between Egyptians and a foreign intruder. Nile Valley, fourth millennium BCE, Louvre Museum, Paris.

The expression used for "martial arts" in modern Greek—following the English derived from Latin—is *polemikes texnes,* the "arts of war." But this is a fallacy. The Greek word for "war," *polemos* (πόλεμος), is a compound term, stemming from the Greek noun for "city," *polis,* and the verb *ollymi,* "to destroy"; in other words, war in Greek means to "destroy a city." Conversely, looking at the Chinese ideogram *wu* (figure 1.3), which today is used internationally to represent the martial arts (*wu shu* is the term for "martial arts" in Chinese), we see that the figure represents a castle. A castle never moves to attack; on the contrary, it is constructed for defensive purposes. Perhaps a better translation of the term *wu shu* would be "methods against warfare."

Therefore it is better to speak of "defensive" or "combative" arts instead of "martial" arts. We will return to this topic in chapter 4 where we will examine the esoteric path inherent to the combative arts. Suffice it to say that the ancient Greeks did not think very highly of Ares, their god of war, who in turn became the Roman Mars, from whom arises the word "martial."

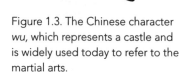

Figure 1.3. The Chinese character *wu*, which represents a castle and is widely used today to refer to the martial arts.

### *The Impact of Bronze*

In addition to the emerging concepts of the duel and personal battle, materials technology offers confirmation of the emergence of the warrior class. The ascendancy of the warrior class in early society is inexorably tied to the dominance of bronze both as a material and a commodity of exchange.

From the beginnings of the third millennium BCE, bronze changed the tide of human history and laid the foundations for the social conditions that led to the authority of the warrior class. The method of processing bronze was a prized secret. In addition, bronze was expensive and sought after. Since the weapons made from this new material were more effective than the stone weapons used until then, bronze weapons were assigned to those who, in practical terms, were more capable of using them. These were the elite of the warrior class, the heroes and demigods of the Bronze Age, the fastest and strongest of ancient society. The Greek Hercules, the Babylonian Gilgamesh, the Jewish Samson, and the Indian Arjuna were all of the class of the male warrior elite, heroes who, as we shall see later, fought with divine force.

Indeed, it seems that the appearance of bronze weapons coincided with the gradual disappearance of the matriarchy. As male kings and heroes became dominant, the female goddesses of the earth were gradually replaced by the male sky gods of the warrior class: Zeus, Indra, Horus, and Thor—all gods of the heavens, of thunder and lightning. Máche replaced spirituality as the driving force in society; smelted bronze, the stones of the earth.

Bronze is an alloy of copper, bearing roughly 5 to 10 percent tin. Copper was used long before the Bronze Age began, without effecting social change, hence it is to the second main component of bronze—tin—that we must look in order to get an idea of the extent of trade at that time. Copper knives and hatchets had become popular throughout the ancient world beginning in the fifth millennium BCE, but due to the relatively soft density of copper, they were more status symbols than functionally useful objects. In fact, good quality obsidian weapons and tools were much more effective than copper ones (so was well-napped flint, for that matter). As copper metallurgy improved, so did copper axes and knives, but it was not until the discovery of bronze that metal weapons suddenly became de rigueur. Bronze weapons were far, far better than their stone counterparts—and everyone wanted them.

There are Bronze Age mines for copper malachite ore in France, Britain, Ireland, Spain, Slovakia, Yugoslavia, Austria, and Cyprus. But tin does not occur naturally in the Mediterranean, or in Egypt or Mesopotamia. There are some minor deposits in Anatolia, Italy, and Spain—but where did the tin come from that was used in, say, the third millennium bronzes found in the royal graves of Ur and in the city of Susa? We know now that Near Eastern cities imported tin from the East, most likely from Afghanistan, and that trans-European commerce exploited tin deposits in Cornwall, England, and southern Brittany in the early second millennium BCE.

The archaeological record tells us that by the fifteenth century BCE, organized, long-distance trading was established throughout the world.* This trade linked the far reaches of northern Europe to the southern shores of India, and, I suspect, to places far beyond. We know, for example, that all the amber found in Mycenaean and Minoan Greece is of Baltic origin—and we know that ebony and hippopotamus and elephant

---

*This is now the official position of the European Union: Council of Europe. "The Roots of Odysseus" in *Gods and Heroes of Bronze Age Europe* [a museum exhibition catalog]. Bonn: Hatje/Conte, Ostfildern-Ruit, 1999, 103–5.

ivory were moved throughout the world in considerable quantities. And royalty in ancient times often exchanged valuable gifts from far-away locales—hence the presence of Near Eastern seals and jewelry in Mycenaean Greek graves, and vice versa.

Furthermore, trade was democratic, not something reserved just for royalty. As early as the third millennium BCE, before the Bronze Age proper, quality stones for use in tools and weapons were traded liberally throughout Europe and the Near East. Obsidian from the Mediterranean, dolerite from Brittany, and flint from England, Germany, and Poland flowed around the continent. Pottery was traded from east to west and south to north, and Lebanese wood specifically became known widely as a reliable construction material.

## Swords and Warriors

Beyond materials, cultural innovations also made their way from place to place: the yoke plow, alcoholic beverages, and the bridle are all prime examples. One other artifact, something most important to this text, made its way through ancient lands: the sword. It is the journey of the sword that provides strong archeological evidence of the existence of the warrior elite, primarily because early swords were essentially dueling weapons—and the duel was an important concept for these men, both in times of war and peace.

Though we will see that ritual duels with weapons took place almost five millennia earlier, the first archeological evidence of a mock duel with simulated weaponry comes from Egypt, in a reference to ceremonial stick-fighting dated to 2300 BCE. A later depiction (dated to 1400 BCE) shows two warriors dueling with sticks held in their right hands and second pieces of wood attached to their left forearms as shields (figure 1.4). The reference indicates that such duels took place almost a millennium earlier. Though it is doubtful that the first swords were manufactured in Egypt, the concept of the nonlethal duel is well represented in ancient Egyptian culture, and Egyptian military tactics may have led to the development of the sword in the first place.

From the sixth millennium BCE onward, elite warriors fought out their wars, dueling, for the most part, among themselves. Their principal weapons were the bow and javelin; their primary close-quarter (CQ) combat weapon was the spear. But bronze knives became important when they became available in the third millennium. We can surmise

Figure 1.4. Mock duel in honor of the God Horus. From Grave 19 at Thebes, Ancient Egypt, 1400 BCE. (Drawing by Sir Richard Francis Burton, from the *Book of the Sword*.)

that, due to cost and logistics, javelin points and arrowheads continued to be made of stone or bone until bronze became more commonplace. Close-quarter combat weaponry, however, quickly turned to bronze, inasmuch as bronze weapons were more effective and durable. Bronze weapons also became a prize, to be taken by the victor of a duel to the death.

Because bronze knives were used within CQ combat range, and strength played a decisive role in battles, warriors of lesser size and strength looked for methods of victory based on technique, speed, and the delivery of a blow with precise timing. By the third millennium BCE, it is clear that combat techniques that took advantage of the opponent's weak spots had been developed (millennia later Homer would call these techniques *kerdea*, "methods used to win"). It is interesting that the bronze ax and the shield were the principal weapons of CQ combat at the time; perhaps metallurgical limitations and material logistics played a role in this choice.

In Europe, together with the classic single-edged and double-edged hatchet, a unique new weapon was developed. This was a bronze double-edged knife attached perpendicularly to a long wooden shaft, forming a weapon that would come to be called a "crow bill" by

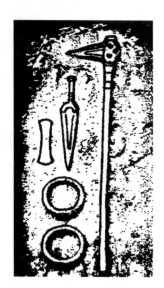

Figure 1.5. A warrior's grave at Koscian, Poland. We can see the classic type of broad ax, a sword, and a crow bill with a long pole. Lěki Male, Unêtice culture, twentieth to nineteenth centuries BCE, Museum Archeologiczne, Poznan. (Drawing based on museum photograph.)

modern hoplologists. Such examples have been unearthed in Ireland, England, central Europe, and the Balkans, and were prevalent from 2300 to 1600 BCE (figure 1.5). A possible use for this weapon may have been to reach over an opponent's shield to strike while, at the same time, on the return stroke, hooking onto the lip and forcing it down so that another man might attack with hatchet or spear.

In Egypt, the war hatchet was designed to be broad and wide, and perhaps signaled the eventual development of the sword, once metallurgical limitations were overcome (figure 1.6). The broad bronze war hatchet of Egypt was developed with one purpose in mind: to split shields in two and then to do the same to the opponent.

Inspired perhaps by Egypt, the weapons craftsmen of Mesopotamia created the first swords over the next few centuries. Curved and made of forged bronze, they resembled scythes. These weapons no doubt had a very specific purpose, since the warriors' principal weapons remained the spear and bow. For the most part, noblemen and kings owned swords. In addition, these specific weapons were probably not very resistant to impact. A Sumerian carved relief from the third millennium BCE (sometime between 2400 and 2100 BCE) shows a warrior holding a hatchet and the sword-scythe of the Middle East.*

Representations of bronze swords with curving blades dating from the third millennium have also been found at the early Babylonian dynastic site in Tello. This indicates that Babylonian metallurgists may have been the first to come up with a technique for casting larger quantities of bronze, and that their bursars were the first to decipher the logistics of moving and refining large quantities of tin. In a tomb at Byblos in Lebanon, dating to the early eighteenth century BCE, examples of the real thing—swords in good condition—were first uncovered in the late nineteenth century. Quite a few have been found since then, more notably in Luristan in modern Iraq.†

The existence of these weapons is important for two reasons: first, they prove that bronze could be processed to make weapons of this sort beginning in the third millennium, and second (and more notably), they suggest a transition in the policy of warfare to include personal

---

*Time-Life Books, *The Enterprise of War*.

†In the beginning of 2003, in Turkey, a 5,000-year-old sword was discovered. It is possible that all the aforementioned dates will have to be pushed back by roughly a millennium, or that sword combat began elsewhere than stipulated here.

Figure 1.6. Egyptian soldiers with shields and characteristic broad hatchets, which may have led to the development of the sword. (Drawing by Sir Richard Francis Burton from the *Book of the Sword*.)

close-quarter encounters, or duels, with expensive bladed weapons. In essence, these swords would not have been particularly useful in the melee of Bronze Age combat (the spear and the bow were much more effective weapons); they only make sense if ritual dueling coexisted with uncontrolled warfare en masse.

These curved swords of the Middle East disappeared rather quickly, however, due to the emergence of a defensive countermeasure (and concomitant technological achievement): bronze armor, or armor made of processed leather reinforced with bronze plates. According to our current understanding, warriors began to use bronze armor during the seventeenth and sixteenth centuries BCE; this was when the standardized double-edged swords of the Bronze Age made their first appearance. Most people around the world would recognize these swords today, as their function hasn't changed: they were basically designed for the thrust. The tip of this sword could slide between the plates of armor and wound an adversary, while the curved edge of its predecessor could not cut through bronze plates.

From western Asia the sword quickly made its way into Europe by means of Anatolia, the Aegean, and mainland Greece. By the sixteenth century BCE, the bronze double-edged sword, waspwaisted and rapier-like, had a similar shape and make throughout all of continental Europe,

Figure 1.7. Double-edged sword of the Bronze Age. The shape and style of these swords was the same from Iran to England and from Egypt to Sweden during this period, a by-product of the cultural interaction caused by the global trade in copper and tin. This particular blade is from Hungary, from the Hadjúsámson area, and dates to the sixteenth century BCE. (Drawing based on a museum photograph.)

western Asia, and the Mediterranean basin. It was a treasured artifact whose mythos was to far surpass that of its predecessors: the spear, the bow, and the ax.

By the seventeenth century BCE then, Greeks, Egyptians, Mesopotamians, the tribes of northern Europe, the peoples of the Middle East—more or less everyone—used the same type of weaponry. This observation is of utmost importance, because, if the weaponry in a given geographic area (crisscrossed by commercial trade routes supporting the copious movement of merchandise) was the same, *it stands to reason that the use of such weapons in those lands must have been essentially the same*. For example, people today shoot the same pistol in the same manner in Sweden as they do in South Africa.

We will use this conclusion to support our reconstruction of the combative techniques and submission wrestling found in further chapters; this reconstruction is based on an archaeological record collected from many lands over a time scale encompassing millennia. The time scale involved is not a fallacy, for the simple reason that the techniques and methods of individual close-quarter combat did not change over the period described by the archaeological record presented in this text.

For personal reasons, we would like to emphasize a position that will displease those Greeks with ethnocentric tendencies: the double-edged sword did not constitute a prerogative or creation of the Mycenaean Greeks. Rather, it was a product of all the ancient cultures of the Bronze Age in general. Though it is clear that the Mycenaeans used amber from Britain and tin from Afghanistan, the belief that they were the center of civilization and trade, and the fathers of the sciences of their time, is wishful thinking. Accordingly, in an attempt to maintain rationalism, we would dissuade the reader from thinking of these swords as "Mycenaean" despite the fact that this has been a longstanding tendency in Greece and in Greco-centric circles.

In essence, *"The history of the sword is the history of humanity."* This dynamic phrase was used by the great British explorer, archaeologist, and warrior Sir Richard Francis Burton in 1884, in the prologue to his classic work, *The Book of the Sword*. His observation is not without a considerable quantity of truth. Despite our transition to an age of technological warfare, this phrase continues to be timely: the romantic image of the sword has not faded in its appeal. In times of war, for instance, the defeated general will give up his sword to the victor even today. The kings and nobility of Europe and the East, though they no longer have their old political power, still maintain considerable social influence, and the sword continues to support their symbolic role. The queen of England continues to knight those she deems worthy with her sword.

The etymology of the word *sword* is lost in the depths of time. Most likely, however, the word derives from the Egyptian S-F-T (𓏭𓂧𓏭), which was pronounced *seft* or *sfet*. In Mesopotamia, the sword was called *sibiru* (which may well be related to the Greek *xiphos,* pronounced *kseefos*),* as well as *sapara* and *sapata*. The reader may, therefore, using a little imagination, readily find the root of most words that identify the sword (the ancient Greek σπάθη, *spáthi,* the Latin *spatha,* the Arabic *sayf,* the German *schwert,* the English words *sword* and *saber,* and so on) in the Egyptian S-F-T and its Mesopotamian equivalents. This etymology has a special meaning, for it determines the dissemination of the sword as a weapon of choice, which must also be related to its manner of use.

The development and diffusion of the sword in its various forms testifies to the existence of the combative arts in all of the lands where the sword was found, for the simple reason that it would be pointless for expensive dueling weapons of this sort to exist without a strategic and precise method of use. And since, in the seventeenth century BCE, the same weapons were in use from Iran to England and from Egypt to Sweden, we can surmise that the movements and the techniques of their martial arts were similar or identical. This conclusion is supported by our study of ancient depictions, which demonstrate that the martial art of the elite Bronze Age warriors was worldwide in its distribution, and was extremely similar to today's Eastern martial arts that were developed on the basis of combat in armor, such as the art of *jujutsu* that has become known worldwide today and was cultivated by the samurai warrior class of medieval Japan.

In summary, heroes, warriors, and "great kings" existed from one end of the ancient world to the other. The widespread trade in bronze and tin during the Bronze Age, and the similarity of armor and weapons ranging from Britain to faraway Luristan, tell us that a common

---

*Incidentally, the first record we have of the word *xiphos* is the Mycenaean *qi-si-pe-e* found in the Linear B tablets from Pylos.

culture, combative and otherwise, had been established through the ancient world, and that the martial arts—pammachon—were central to this culture's dissemination.

After conducting our research—during which we examined ancient depictions of martial arts from the Mediterranean—we thought it would be of interest to compare the same techniques with those displayed in surviving medieval European close-quarter combat manuals from different countries. We found that the depictions of techniques in the *Flos Duellatorum* by the Italian Fiore de Liberi (1409), *Fechtbuch aus dem Jahre 1467* by the German Hans Talhoffer, and *Codex Wallerstein* (circa 1470) were identical with the ancient depictions, going back all the way to the third millennium BCE. They confirm that the demands and movements of pammachon, for all the peoples of the earth, have not changed since roughly the third millennium BCE, and hence, its practice remains timeless.

# 2

FROM COMBAT
TO COMPETITION

## Pammachon to Pankration

Depictions found at the Egyptian graves of Beni Hasan, most of which date to 2000 BCE, allow us a glimpse into some basic truths regarding the martial arts. On the one hand, these frescoes differentiate ritual athletic competition (combat "sports") from actual warfare: they display a broad range of submission wrestling techniques, drawn in parallel to, yet distinctly separate from, scenes of battle. On the other hand, they make it relatively clear that the best way for warriors to train for conditions of real combat was through the combat sports. The frescoes at Beni Hasan portray athletic combat sports thirteen hundred years before the Olympic games were established in Greece. It is highly likely then that, in addition to the martial arts, the practice of bloodless ritual dueling—through combat sports such as boxing and wrestling—was widespread throughout the Mediterranean and the Middle East beginning from the Neolithic Age.

This distinction between the techniques of actual combat—martial arts—and athletic competition is an essential one. We mentioned that the words máche (combat) and máchaera (blade) stem from the same concept—conflict between two or more combatants with deadly, close-quarter weapons: knives, hatchets, swords, or spears. Naturally, the martial arts of the period should have taught the use of and defense against these weapons, otherwise what would have been the reason for their existence? The term pammachon was officially used before the enactment of the Olympic games in 776 BCE.* We may conclude that pammachon was the way fighters fought, whether armed or unarmed. We can also suggest that pammachon was a training method for fighters in the framework of their preparation for armed battle in actual battlefields.

Over time the martial arts underwent a transformation in which a more technical, regulated form of combat sports evolved. This was perhaps related to the role played by the martial arts in religious worship from ancient times. In chapter 3 we will study the pediments from the Parthenon (the chief temple of Athena in Athens) and the temple of Apollo at Vasses, which today can be found in the British Museum, and we will see that they almost exclusively depict scenes of pammachon. Similarly, the scenes of submission grappling and combat sports that come from the graves of Beni Hasan in Egypt have a clear religious foundation. Then again, we should not ignore the fact that all athletic competitions in ancient Greece were in essence religious festivals in honor of a given god—the Olympian, Pythian, Nemean, and Isthmian games, and so forth. The exact correlation, in the context of historical development, between athletic activity and religious ritual is something that bears study in detail.

Yet—beyond gratifying whatever psychological and philosophical need for releasing social stress that ancient societies may have had—combat sports were a solution to an obvious problem (while at the same time giving people the chance to honor their gods). This is the challenge of *safely* training martial arts practitioners, with the goal of developing strength, reflexes, flexibility, precision, and stamina. It is impossible to practice genuine martial arts without instituting regulations. By establishing rules in the contests, the ancients were able to minimize the dangers that are inherent to both the use of weapons and blows with the bare hand to vital points. At the same time they were able to help their warriors train physically, emotionally, and mentally for combat. In contrast with us today, however, *the ancients never forgot the difference between a combat sport and a martial art,* probably because close-quarter combat was a matter of life and death for almost every one of their citizens.

---

*M. B. Poliakoff, *Studies in the Terminology of the Greek Combat Sports*, 2nd ed. (Meisenheim: Beiträge zur Klassichen Philologie, 1986), 146.

This distinction is expressed by the use of a different term to refer to the combat sport: *pankration.* Pankration is a compound word coming from *pan* and *kratos,* meaning: "he who holds everything," one with absolute power or authority. The ancient Greeks attributed the characterization of *pan + kratos* to special cases such as heroes, semi-gods, and gods. *Pankrates* is he who holds everything, according to a commentator on Sophocles. A commentator on Aeschylus wrote that Zeus is called *pankrateus* because he dominates, conquers, and reigns over everybody. Aristophanes in *Thesmophoriasouses* calls Athena *pankrates kore* (omnipotent daughter) of Zeus. They said of Hercules that he had a powerful heart. Later, these titles—*pankrates* and *pantokrator*—were used by the Church, denoting the power of God and Christ.

Within the framework of sports jargon we can say that pankration is a "battle for submission," a contest where each athlete aims to subdue his opponent. In fact, in addition to meaning "strength" and "power," the word *kratos* also means "control" and "submission." * By example, Ares—the god of war whose totem was the vulture—was followed into battle by *Kratos* (domination/control/power) and *Bia* (violence).

Pankration was a combat sport introduced in the Thirty-third Olympiad in 648 BCE with clearly defined rules and restrictions. As such, it differed substantially from the techniques used in combat on battlefields, shown by the literal meaning of the word pammachon: *"I fight in any manner."* In any manner! We cannot say this about pankration athletes, because the way they fought in wrestling grounds was predetermined and controlled by a set of rules. In fact, the sport of pankration—*unarmed combat between two people, during which they exchange blows and perform holds in order to subdue their opponent within an athletic game's framework*—was not much different from the submission wrestling and submission fighting that enjoys worldwide popularity today, beginning with with "no-holds-barred" and "ultimate fighting championship" competitions in the 1990s.

The techniques of this sporting contest were totally different from the technique of the martial art of pammachon, which was based on blows to vital points that directly incapacitated an enemy, or locks and throws that controlled him in such a manner that he no longer presented a threat and could be quickly executed. In pammachon, the methodology and execution

---

*Interestingly enough, the word also means "country" and "government," which places a disturbing slant on politics.

of defensive (or offensive) techniques also took into account the possibility that the enemy was armed, either openly or carrying concealed weapons, and that there could be more than one opponent involved in the battle. The kinesiology of the pammachon practitioner was also the same, whether he was armed or unarmed, wearing armor or unarmored.

For example, pammachon included training with wooden and, subsequently, real weapons. We have seen that the Egyptians practiced ritual stick-fighting in preparation for the sword duel (in fact, Alexander the Great spoke highly of this), and we also know that Roman soldiers trained with wooden weapons. For the classical Greeks, there is no archaeological evidence of this practice (though we could say that lack of evidence does not necessarily mean that wooden weapons were not used for training). We know that the Bronze Age Greeks practiced ritual dueling with weapons *(hoplomachia)*, but we are not quite sure how it was done, and what the rules were, if any—usually it was carried out in religious festivals and funeral games. But it seems that the classical Greeks did not have equivalent practices in their athletic competitions, raising the question of why and how they were discontinued.

Plato in his *Laws* recommends the introduction of hoplomachia to the gymnasium, as necessary for the training of citizens and warriors. But it is not until the third century BCE that the historical record tells us that "fencing" was reintroduced to southwestern Greece (and even then, not to the famed cities of Athens or Sparta). Participants used a short wooden sword, a wooden spear, full metal helmet and shin guards, a wooden shield, and a leather chest protector. Perhaps, following Alexander's conquests, they had evaluated, and were worried about, the military techniques used by other nations of the ancient world.

## HISTORICAL REFERENCES AND TERMINOLOGY

There has been some confusion regarding the distinction between these two terms, in part because the founders of the Olympic games initially gave the name pammachon to the new combat sport (actually pankration) before realizing that they should make a clear distinction between the combat sport and the martial art.* It was not long, however, before

---

*Poliakoff, *Studies in the Terminology of the Greek Combat Sports*, 2nd ed.; and Louis Robert, *L'epigramme Grecque* (Geneva: Entretiens sur l'antiquité classique, 1968).

the official name of the combat sport was changed to pankration. The clear difference between it and the pammachon of the battlefield is reflected by ancient texts.

Aristotle, in *Rhetorics,* mentions that a "wrestler is he who can arrest and hold the other man tightly, a boxer is he who inflicts injuries with blows, and he who fights using both these methods is a pankration athlete." A commentator on Plato gives the following definition of pankration: "This is a contest consisting partially of wrestling and partially of boxing." Plutarch mentions that "pankration is a mixture of wrestling and boxing." According to Philostratos, wrestling, boxing, and pankration were included in the Olympic games for their usefulness in battle, since in Marathon and Thermopylae "after their swords and spears were broken, they achieved a great deal with bare hands; wrestling and pankration proved useful in actual battle." Plutarch confirms this: "All these are not just games, they are also useful in real battle."* Philostratos also points out that it is the best Olympic game: "In Olympia and the Olympic games, the best contest for men is pankration."

In ancient Greece all games were believed to have originated from the gods. According to Plutarch, the ancient Greeks believed that pankration was created by the hero Theseus, who beat the Minotaur using a pankration technique. A commentator on Pindar reports: "Theseus the Athenian, in the Labyrinth, much weaker in strength than the Minotaur, fought with him and won using pankration, as he had no knife." According to Pausanias, pankration was created by the semi-divine hero Hercules. Pindar's commentator mentions that according to Aristotle, the game of pankration was more technical than its previous form and that Leukaros the Akarnanian was considered to be its transformer. Aristotle said that, "Leukaros the Akarnanian was the first to transform pankration into a technical game."

As mentioned earlier, for a martial art to be effective on the battlefield, it must use the same class of movement, whether the fighter is armed or unarmed, either wearing armor or not, whether facing one or multiple opponents. In the Olympic sport of pankration, however, unarmored athletes ended up rolling on the ground 99 percent of the time (the same thing occurs in mixed martial arts contests today). This is the natural outcome of a scuffle between two combatants who are fighting with conventions imposed for their safety, without weapons, and in a restricted space.

---

*Ethics, 639E.

However, it is clear that *it was not feasible for an armored warrior to fight on the ground,* due to the weight of the armor and its rigidity, and due to the danger of being struck by an unseen opponent in the melee!

Therefore, it is obvious to serious hoplologists that the true martial art of the ancient Greeks and the sport of pankration were *not* one and the same. It would be like comparing *yoroi kumiuchi,* the battlefield martial art of the medieval samurai of Japan, with competitive judo today—the two are only superficially similar. The boundaries and the goals of one differ from those of the other. However one may look at them, combat sports are by their nature one thing, and martial arts another.

This is clearly demonstrated by a closer look at technique. The series of movements that is depicted in the photographs (A–H) show the classic mounted position used in submission grappling today. In combat sports, it is undoubtedly a position that allows for control and ready submission of the opponent, and if we refer to the archeological record we will see that it has always been this way.

In combat, however, where the possibility of bladed weapons being used is present, this position is especially vulnerable, as we can see (A–F). The abdominal area and the combatant's leg are straightforward targets for the knife (A–C). The defender cannot easily control the knife, as in doing so, he would expose his eyes to gouging—a catch-22 situation (D–F). In addition, as we can see (G–H) even if there is no knife, this position potentially allows the opponent to seize the defender's genitals.

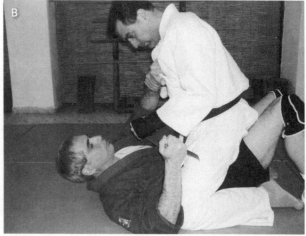

In arts clearly developed for battle, the main objective is to eliminate one's own weak points in every movement, while taking advantage of the opponent's. The adversary is typically controlled in a face-down position, for example, in which the defender does not expose vulnerable areas to attack. When, in fact, the opponent is detained in a face-up position, the "hold down," made popular by combat sports since ancient times, is indeed important for battlefield conditions. The point of holding your adversary down is, sadly, to retain him in an immobile position long enough for one of your own to come along and thrust something sharp and nasty into a vital point, or until you can do so yourself. Thus, combat sports, since ancient times, did indeed reflect training for conditions of combat (though please note that the "hold down" does not necessarily have to do with forcing an opponent to submission as in mixed martial arts today).

It has also become accepted today, even by the most ardent supporters of submission fighting and mixed martial arts, that that these arts are designed for applications in situations of individual contests, one on one. If you are dealing with more than one adversary, it is not a very good strategy to go to the ground with the intention of defeating the first opponenet, as you will most likely expose yourself to the attacks of the others. In addition, there are circumstances, such as when the adversary is carrying a weapon, when the techniques of a combat sport must be completely modified to insure the safety of the defender.

In military terminology, the distinction between combat sports and the martial arts would refer to "lines of drift." Lines of drift are natural or man-made features that tend to lead people (or animals) toward a given direction. Examples of these are bridges, game trails, and roads. Normally people are apt to follow lines of drift when moving: we sacrifice freedom of movement in exchange for ease of movement along a line of drift. Simply put, faster and more convenient routes of transportation such as highways are preferable to game trails, though the actual distance from point to point may be greater along a highway. Military personnel, however, do not follow lines of drift in combat, because this is where, more often than not, ambushes are established. The examples above, involving a bladed weapon or exposed vulnerable points when an opponent is in the mounted position, are similar. Exposing a vulnerable point to attack is similar to establishing a line of drift, hence it is a condition that one must be aware of during combat.

The mounted position described in the paragraphs above does indeed expose, for moments in time, vulnerable areas of the body to attack and it would be best, in an uncontrolled environment, to avoid such possibilities. That having been said, there is no guarantee that a defender (or an assailant) will be able to reach a weak point when faced with a skilled opponent. Even though combat sports have rules forbidding the practitioners from attacking these points, there is also no doubt that practitioners of combat sports today *tend to be considerably more skilled than their counterparts in the traditional martial arts,* simply because practicing with a resisting partner allows for the development of higher levels of skill.

## PREPARING FOR COMBAT

Although the differences between pammachon and pankration are clear, the right training for martial arts practitioners is incomplete without the inclusion of combat sports. If one had not become accustomed to competition through sports, he might be found lacking physically, emotionally, and intellectually when he took part in battle. This is testified to by the *Codex Wallerstein* (a fifteenth-century combat manual), which refers to the difference between combat sports and the martial arts:

> Doch so ist ein yeder krancker ringer im ernsten einem starken zu gleichen hat er pehentikait und mass kampfstuck und mordstuck enpfor genomen aber mit gesellen ringen so hacz der starck alzeit enpfor doch so wirt dy kunst gelopt vor ritter und knechten fur allew ding.
>
> Translation: Although a weak fighter in a serious combat can be equal to a strong opponent if he has previously learned agility, reach, fighting tricks, and killing tricks, in a friendly combat, strength always has the advantage; in spite of this, the art of fighting *[wrestling]* is praised by knights and squires above all things.*

---

*Translation by Gregorz Zabinski and Bartlomiej Walczak, from their *Codex Wallerstein*. The reference to "wrestling" is mine, as I believe the author is trying to distinguish combat from combat sports. Zabinski, Grzegorz, Walczak, and Bartlomiej, *Codex Wallerstein: A Medieval Fighting Book from the Fifteenth Century on the Longsword, Falchion, Dagger, and Wrestling* (Boulder, Colorado: Paladin Press, 2001).

There are also historical anecdotes that demonstrate that advanced skill in a combat sport allowed the competitor to win in actual combat. For instance, there is the well-known duel of Dioxippos the Athenian and Koragos the Macedonian. In a state of drunkenness, the Macedonian challenged the Athenian to a duel. Dioxippos had won the pankration competition at the Olympiad in 336 BCE. King Alexander himself set the date for the duel and thousands of soldiers gathered for the event. Koragos appeared in full armor, in contrast to Dioxippos, who appeared in the nude, oiled like an athlete, and holding a club like Hercules.

Koragos first threw a javelin at him, but Dioxippos avoided it, and so Koragos tried to stab him with his spear. Dioxippos avoided the thrust and broke the spear in two with his club. Desperate, Koragos tried to stab him with a knife, but the Athenian grabbed his right hand with his own left, breaking his balance, and then knocked him off both feet and threw him to the ground. The winner, Dioxippos rested his foot on his opponent's throat and raised his club, looking out at the audience as does the winner in the pankration. Apparently, Dioxippos had knowledge of both pammachon and pankration, which allowed him an easy victory.

And yet, the controversy as to whether combat sports are appropriate for training warriors has lasted for centuries. Euripides, for example, in his work *Autolykos,* teases professional athletes:

> Name one renowned wrestler, one swift runner, one champion discus-thrower, one expert boxer who has served his country by winning laurels. Do they drive the enemy out of the fatherland by throwing the discus, or do they break the row of the enemy's shields with their kicks? No man is so mad as to do this when facing the horror of deadly steel.

In the *Iliad* we find the example of Epeios, who, though an unbeaten boxer, did not enjoy great esteem among his peers in actual combat. General Philopoimen (fourth century BCE), a distinguished wrestler, learned through bitter experience that athletes did not become good warriors, and so forbade his soldiers from taking part in athletic competitions! The philosopher Plato (although a wrestler himself) was against pankration as a means of training warriors, while he supported fencing and training in mass competitions with wooden weapons. On the other hand, King Agesilaus of Sparta, that formidable warrior, instituted athletic games in Ephesus to keep his soldiers in good shape.*

A second distinction we have to make is that between *war* and *battle* (or *combat*). *Battle,* in this book, refers to combat between two or more adversaries with close-quarter combat weapons such as knives or swords. *War* is technological, a science unto itself, and is not necessarily tied to notions of archaic and classic combat, as we present them here. In the Greek battle of Sphakteria in 425 BCE, for example, the Spartans surrendered to the Athenians (for the first time in their history) because their armored warriors could not close with the lightly armed auxiliaries of the Athenians, who outflanked them and bombarded them with arrows and stones from a distance, decimating them. Similarly, today skill in close-quarter combat does not necessarily protect a person from bombs dropped by a B-2, or from the 30mm bullets of an Apache helicopter.

Why then should we study close-quarter combat and combat sports? Without going into the benefits of psychosomatic exercise at this point, we could state that, simply, knives, hatchets, and lances continue to be a threat to citizens. In addition, the protective gear and armor that police officers and soldiers wear today is not different in function from that of the armed warriors of the classical and medieval ages. Nothing has changed, in other words, and as a result, both martial arts and combat sports, from a technical point of view, are timely and directly applicable.

## MARTIAL ARTS WEST TO EAST

A popular legend around the world today is that the most prevalent Eastern martial arts (such as karate and many styles of kung fu) are a development of the martial and meditative-respiratory exercises taught by the Zen Patriarch Bodhidharma to the monks of the Buddhist Shaolin temple in Hunan province, China, circa 520 CE.

In the past two decades, ethnocentric circles in Greece (and beyond) have propagated the theory that Shaolin kung fu is an exclusive derivation of a Greek martial art that the supporters of this view have arbitrarily named pankration. This is a documented position on their part: most federations associated with pankration today advertise that the

---

*Michael Poliakoff, *Combat Sports in the Ancient World* (New Haven: Yale University Press, 1987).

martial arts, as a Greek creation *par excellence,* traveled by way of Alexander the Great to the Indian subcontinent, and from there to the Chinese (with the implied supposition that all nations along the way were bereft of martial arts until Alexander's arrival), to provide the impetus for the creation of karate, kung fu, judo, and so forth. This theory, however, can be readily disproved, and discloses a lack of knowledge of the related historical events, battles, and cultural interactions. Sadly, it seems that the people who promote such theories are unaware that Alexander himself considered the combat sport of pankration unsuitable for the training of warriors.*

These assertions do raise the question of whether there is some relationship between the ancient Greek combat sport of pankration and the Shaolin kung fu popularly attributed to the Zen Patriarch. In the appendix we will deal with this question and present a model—based on historical events and the archaeological record—by which a cultural exchange between Greece and China could have taken place over the centuries. At this point, however, we refer to this question only to make another point.

The purpose of this book is to explore the archaic and classical martial arts and combat sports of the ancient Mediterranean in general, and ancient Greece in particular. But in furthering our exploration into what exactly comprises the combat sport of pankration and the martial art of pammachon, it is not our intention to concentrate on this distinction with a Greco-centric bias, but rather to use these two words to specify the divergence of combat sports and martial arts in general. To this end, we will use these ancient Greek words to clarify a distinction that exists in every country on Earth that has developed combat sports and martial arts, or will develop them in the future.

## "THE GAMES BEGIN— OF MOST NOBLE FEATS A TREASURY"

All of the Olympic games of the ancients had their origins in the need for combat training and thus were closely connected to actual battle.

---

*As mentioned by Plutarch in *Alexandros 4.* It is probable that the great general was concerned with bridging the gap between combat sports, the martial arts, and military strategy, as we will see farther on.

The ability to run quickly for short or long distances, to overcome natural obstacles, to strike a distant target with a thrown javelin, to box or wrestle, are all battle-preparation activities. Like pankration, the games of wrestling and boxing began as individual martial skills that became athletic contests over time, and their techniques changed considerably in accord with the spirit of a game and in opposition to actual combat. As athleticism evolved, the combat sports developed their own characteristic traits and skillsets. One indication of this is that in the ancient Olympic games the contestants were nude and in the "heavy" contests—such as wrestling, boxing, and pankration—rubbed their bodies with oil.

After the Olympic games began in 776 BCE, young men trained in sporting contests not only to prepare for war, but in a wider framework of their culture, with the goal of becoming not only ideal fighters but ideal citizens. Still, pankration's origins as a way of training for actual combat could be seen in its early practice in the Olympics: athletes were restricted to the standing, battle-related positions. Thus, prior to the fifth century BCE, artistic representations of athletes show them standing on their feet, fighting with blows and kicks. Similarly, presentations that we are sure depict pammachon show absolutely no fighting on the ground.

However, the distinction between the martial art and the fighting contest remained clear for centuries. Klemes the Alexandrian, for example, the father of the Orthodox Church in the second century CE, mentions the difference between pammachon and pankration, with praise for both. The most significant factor distinguishing pankration from pammachon was the rules that govern the practice of pankration, which in turn determine the techniques, strategies, and tactics of the game.

## RULES

Although the word *pankration* can be translated as "he who holds everything," there were ample restrictive rules. Philostratos mentions that biting was banned in pankration. Plutarch mentions that the genitals, abdomen, and throat were off limits in pankration. Several references to choking and strangulation cases indicate that blows to the neck were also restricted—this is logical, since the intention was not to kill the opponent but to subdue him.

The game ended when one of the contestants declared his submission. Submission was declared in the following two ways:

1. By lifting one finger high up, which we can see in many presentations on pottery; this was also used in wrestling and boxing.
2. By striking on the shoulder (tapping out), a move by which one's resignation is declared even today in combat sports.

In figure 2.1 we can see a depiction of a technique forbidden in pankration, and a judge intervening to stop it. The presence of judges was not superficial; it was essential, as they had the authority to intervene by hitting any contestant who violated one of the rules with a stick, to offer the fighters relief from exhaustion, or to protect one of the contestants if he looked pale and weak, rather than in good health as he should be!

The mightiest rule was the unwritten law to "Compete Nobly" *(eugenês ámilla),* which characterized the athletic contests of the Olympic games. So, in spite of the hardships and rigor of the game, during which the athletes frequently reached or even exceeded their limits, only one accidental death in a pankration match was recorded in ancient Olympia. This death was most likely caused by the victim and not by his opponent. The victim

Figure 2.1. Typical example of forbidden technique. The athlete on the right attacks his opponent's eyes, unable to free himself from his opponent's hold. Red amphora, British Museum. (Drawing based on photograph from the museum.)

was Arrichion, who was proclaimed the winner of the contest after his death, because he had forced his opponent to resign by snapping his ankle, while he himself was held in a strangulation hold by his rival. Arrichion, prompted by his trainer, preferred to die rather than resign the game.

It is worth noting that there were fewer injuries in pankration than in boxing. This is shown by the following reports from various authors. Artemidoros mentions in his work *The Book of Dreams* that "pankration has the same properties as boxing, but it has no injuries." Michael Poliakoff writes: "The ancient Greeks did not consider it more dangerous than boxing, because a man who wanted to compete both in pankration and boxing chose to compete in pankration first, in order to avoid injuries." The fact that pankration was a safer game than boxing leads us to three conclusions:

1. There were many more restrictive rules in pankration.
2. Most likely athletes on the ground fought using holds and locks rather than blows, with the aim of leading their opponent into a critical joint lock causing submission.
3. Although boxing and pankration shared a common goal—forcing the opponent to resign—they used different means to achieve it. To be specific, if a man uses only his fists to subdue his opponent, he will most likely injure him, because, unlike the body, the head has no muscle tissue to protect it. As submission wrestling was allowed in pankration, a finishing joint lock often prevailed as a way to force submission, which ideally would have an immediate effect, much as in today's mixed martial arts contests.

All these restrictive rules obviously did not exist on the battlefield, where fighters could use any method to eliminate and not just subdue their enemy.

## CONSTITUTING ELEMENTS OF PANKRATION

An examination of the elements characterizing the game of pankration in ancient Olympia will enable us to draw interesting conclusions concerning the techniques of the game as well as the development of specific physical properties.

## Strength and Technique

*Initially, strong and large athletes had the advantage in
the pursuit of victory. With their weight and strength they
could subdue their opponent. As time passed, around
the seventh to sixth century BCE, stamina, with added
strength, patience, and technique, created the ideal
pankration athletes.*

TH. B. YIANNAKIS, *ANCIENT KNOWLEDGE*,
*PHILOSOPHY OF COMPETITION*

There were no weight categories in pankration, which gave bigger and
stronger athletes the advantage. This is supported by some other parameters as we shall see. In the game of pankration, strength and size could
overcome a smaller opponent's better technical skills. In the battlefield,
however, the effective use of weapons demanded refined technique and
correct timing, regardless of strength and size. Weapons were ideal
"equalizers." The same applies today. Good soldiers—in addition to their
good physical condition, which is a "must"—base their excellence on the
correct use of weapons and on strategy, not on physical strength.

## The Ground and Restricted Mobility

The ground on which pankration took place was dug-up sand, called
a *skamma* (which simply means "dug up"). The reason for this was
to allow the fighters to fight and fall without getting injured but also
because this kind of terrain brought about restrictions in mobility that
duplicated the conditions of the actual battlefield while wearing armor.
This leads us to some useful comparisons between pankration and the
martial arts of the East.

    The difficulty involved with moving on dug-up sand is clear to any-
one who has tried. Lateral moves are especially difficult, which mirrors
the fact that human beings move forward much more frequently than
sideways in an actual melee. In the game of pankration (as in other
fighting contests such as wrestling and boxing) a straight move was the
prevailing move (in contrast to modern contests). The type of step made
popular today by sixteenth- to nineteenth-century traditional Japanese
martial arts—where the student glides on his feet without picking them
up in order to enhance his balance, has been developed for use *inside*
buildings on *tatami* (rice-plant fiber) mats; however, it has no practical

application in a natural environment where one is more likely to trip over a root or stone using same.

Considering the restrictions in mobility and the size advantage, pankration athletes approached each other with impetus—mostly in a linear fashion—to quickly reduce the distance between them. This resulted in a powerful collision between two well-prepared athletes, whose physical capabilities were extremely well developed; this "collision" is somewhat reminiscent of Japanese *sumo*.

### Avoidance and Blocks

Avoidance—especially at close range where hand blows were typically used—was executed by a short move of the body and bending of the knees, while blocks were enhanced and executed in two ways: a) hand blows on the limbs of the opponent; b) "refined (soft) avoidance" along with penetrating moves aimed at capturing the offensive limb. One should imagine the delicate parries of Western fencing when visualizing this approach; please note that this type of parry was characteristic of pammachon, and was brought into pankration as a result. Avoiding the opponent using long steps or extraordinarily deep stances was difficult. Therefore the timing of the athletes had to be excellent and very precise.

The athletes guarded their heads in combat position by placing their hands relatively high up (keep in mind that "heel of the hand" and "base of the fist" blows were common, unlike boxing today). However, in order to be ready to hit or hold their opponents at will, pankration athletes used a "looser" position than boxers, who had to guard their heads more carefully and continuously.

## ATHLETICISM IN THE HELLENISTIC ERA

Although these rules and the techniques that arose as a result of these rules characterized pankration throughout its history, other aspects changed over time, particularly after the onset of the Hellenistic era (323–146 BCE). Not only pankration, but all athleticism in the Hellenistic era followed the general course of Hellenism itself. Athletic idealism, born in the ancient cities of classical Greece, reached its summit and, with the conquests of Alexander the Great and the founding of Hellenistic kingdoms, went outside Greece itself. Wherever Hellenism made inroads, traditional athletic settings such as gymnasiums, wrestling rings, and stadiums were created, not only in the new cities built by Alexander, but even in small, remote villages.

This expansion of athleticism and the facilities that supported it was due to several factors: changing political, economic, and social conditions; the appeal that the Panhellenic festivities, especially the Olympics, had for the entire ancient world; and the ambition of the kings of Hellenistic states and other civil authorities to enhance their reputation and legacy. New games—in addition to those that took place between the Olympiads—were started, which attracted worthy athletes and aroused ardent interest among the people. At the same time, the games became more of a show, increasingly disconnected from the religious festivals that were their origin. Their main characteristic trait was their opulence, which was the opposite of the simplicity of older times, and the attention given to providing entertainment to the spectators.

## Professional Athleticism

The great Panhellenic games were originally *stephanêtes,* meaning that the prizes were mere flower wreaths, but starting in the fifth century BCE, various cities honored the winners by offering them gifts of money or other rewards that could be exchanged for money. The phenomenon of athletes competing for money increased during the Hellenistic era and there was no way to stop it. Professional athletes were not an isolated phenomenon, but a result of the changes in the political, economic, and social life of the Greeks; their existence was also closely connected to the evolution of athleticism, that is, with the improvement of the terms of competitions, the specialization of the athletes themselves, and more "professional" performances geared toward amusing the crowd.

With the emergence of professional athletes, professional trainers also appeared, promising great performance and distinction to gifted young men with good physical qualities, and to their parents, provided they followed their hard training program. Motivated by the promise of considerable financial rewards and great privileges, young athletes turned professional, neglecting their general education. This was contrary to the general purpose of athletics ("A Sound Mind in a Sound Body") and is reminiscent of what has happened in the modern age.

# PANKRATION IN THE ROMAN EMPIRE

The period following the enslavement of Greece by the Romans in 146 BCE was critical for athleticism and the athletic ideal. Economic, moral, and social decadence was prevalent. Most local games were terminated and the Panhellenic games withered. However, two factors helped to keep the athletic ideal alive during these difficult years for Hellenism. The first was the glamour of the Panhellenic games. The Romans—in spite of their contempt for athleticism and the athletic endeavors of the Greeks—did not abolish them, perhaps after considering the political benefits they could derive from them. The second factor was the gymnasiums—centers of athletic, intellectual, spiritual, and social activities which were so important to life in the Greek cities. With whatever autonomy was allowed them by the Romans, the Greeks continued to gather at their gymnasiums.

Over time, professional unions developed around the gymnasiums, contributing to the expansion of professional athleticism. In effect, there was a blossoming of athleticism overall, but one that was perhaps superficial, differing substantially from the athletic practices that had been closely connected to religion and the heroes of the past. In the Roman era, athletic events became glamorous shows, attracting fans from East and West, from all ends of the vast Roman Empire. Stadiums became huge in order to accommodate the great number of spectators. The tastes of this public were influenced by the preferences of the Romans, who loved not only tough contests such as boxing, wrestling, and pankration, but also bloody ones, like gladiator duels and fights against wild animals. Money was the only motive for the training of such athletes.

As mentioned earlier, pankration's origins as training for actual combat left their mark on its practice during its first one hundred to two hundred years in ancient Olympia. The aim of the athletes was to beat their opponent quickly, if possible avoiding any fighting while lying on the ground. However, as athleticism became more professional, the strategy and tactics of pankration also transformed, not only in Olympia but in other Panhellenic games as well. During the Roman era, when professional athletes could earn both wealth and fame, the game of pankration became characterized by the extended duration of the contest on the ground. Athletes did not care to finish the game quickly, since their purpose was not to prepare for war, but to obtain financial gains and entertain the spectators. The practice of pankration also became increasingly specialized.

Undoubtedly pankration was the most complete fighting contest between two contestants from its first appearance in Olympia in 648 BCE until its official disappearance (in 364 CE or 393 CE). Today it is once again becoming the same for two unarmed combatants, given the resurgence of the sport in its modern form of mixed martial arts. This book will not expand into a detailed analysis of the history of pankration—there are academic sources and historical studies analyzing this subject extensively. Instead, we shall attempt to explain pankration as a contest and its techniques as developed throughout history, based on the existing archaeological evidence.

# 3

# ANALYSIS OF THE TECHNIQUES OF PANKRATION

In this chapter we shall present the techniques of the combat sport of pankration, while referencing the wider context of the martial arts (pammachon) of the ancient Mediterranean world from which the combat sport originated. Each technique will be represented by an ancient Greek, Egyptian, or Roman depiction of the move, either on pottery or on a frieze, mosaic, or sculpture. The reasons that we freely use depictions from various peoples and empires in the Mediterranean throughout different periods in time are twofold:

1. Given the proven commercial and cultural relations these realms had, beginning with the Bronze Age, we find it highly unlikely that a concomitant diffusion of martial arts and/or combat sports skills did not take place (and we are indifferent in this book as to its direction).

2. We believe that these skills and techniques are universal in nature in any case, and have their roots in the Neolithic period of human development. The representations of ancient technique found in these pages will be followed by a step-by-step breakdown of an identical modern-day move accompanied by sequential photographs of combatants performing it. This presentation also includes

a detailed look at the kinesiology, the knowledge of anatomy, and principles of mechanics implied in these movements. It makes it clear that this tradition has survived remarkably intact since the heyday of ancient Greek civilization, and this is a logical conclusion. There is nothing new in combat—people have been trying to kill each other with traditional weapons for millennia—and the combat sports that provide a training ground for same, have always reflected this reality.

In the study that follows, we refer to combat sports as pankration, and to the martial arts as pammachon, whether the depictions are Egyptian, Mesopotamian, Greek, or Roman; it is our intention to refer to these arts and sports within the general context of the ancient world, and not strictly the Hellenic world. We consider depictions in which warriors defend themselves against mythological creatures (such as centaurs) as *pammachon,* since it is obvious that the artist is not rendering an athletic competition but a scene of actual combat. It is worth noting that in such scenes the fighters are never portrayed grappling on the ground. Some depictions that we have included could be described as either pammachon or pankration, and in these cases we do not differentiate the two, while others are clearly pankration (submission fighting) or boxing, and are labeled as such.

## COMBAT RANGES

During a pankration contest, all kinds of blows and holds were allowed (with very few exceptions), making it the only fighting contest that included all four of the combat ranges typical of combat sports. These four ranges are distinguished by the distance between the fighters and the techniques that are applied in each case. The ranges are:

1. **The Kicking Range:** from around four and a half to five feet; in which kicks are exchanged.
2. **The Boxing Range:** approximately three feet; where hand blows are dealt.
3. **The Entrapment Range:** about twenty inches; in which limb and body holds are executed. Knee, elbow, and head blows are also included.

4. **The Wrestling Range:** less than twenty inches; where—after capturing or engulfing the opponent—holds, throws, lifts, sweeps, and submission/immobilization of the opponent are executed.

## *Special Techniques in Each Combat Range*

Pankration athletes were trained in each combat range. After having fully understood one range, they proceeded to the next range, ultimately advancing to the unification of the ranges. This does not mean that they had learned everything involved with each range's technique. On the contrary, they restricted their techniques to a minimum number during training in order to better obtain correct technique and balance in the next range—that is, in the beginning they did not allow their students to specialize in any one range. More specifically, in the Kicking Range they used only one or two kicks and never kicked above the waist. In the Boxing Range, hooking punches were not preferred except when on the ground, or after capturing the opponent in a lock or hold. In the Wrestling Range, many of the throws and takedowns used in the game of wrestling were undesirable and harmful in pankration.

The inclusion of all four combat ranges makes it clear that pankration was a complicated game. At first glance the designation of techniques to be applied may seem clear, as determined by whether the athletes were standing or rolling on the ground and according to the individual combat range. However, it is far more complicated in an actual fight, because the transfer from one range to another is usually fast and indistinguishable, and because, for example, an athlete fallen on the ground could kick his opponent, depending on the distance between them. In any given contest, the sequence of technical applications would naturally develop in the course of the game, according to the capabilities of the athletes.

# Standing Combat

The first two ranges, the Kicking Range and the Boxing Range, pertain to standing combat, which, as noted earlier, prevailed in the first couple of hundred years of Olympic pankration competitions.

## THE KICKING RANGE

### Principles and Aims

In both pankration and pammachon there is one kind of kick: the front kick to the body or the legs of the opponent, never to the head. Ancient Greeks, along with all Mediterranean peoples, were realists: they knew that an opponent could easily neutralize a high kick and gain an advantage over anyone foolish enough to try it. This was equally true on the battlefield as in athletic competition (you can't kick high while wearing armor). Therefore, high kicks were excluded from both their martial arts and their combat sports. This was not because of lack of knowledge, but by choice.

So, in the Kicking Range, the *front kick* prevails, but with specific targets and goals in mind, as we shall proceed to explain. A basic argument in favor of the front kick is the minimal risk it entails for the athlete executing it. It is easy for a man to perform such a kick while maintaining his balance and preserving a stable erect position for confronting his opponent.

### Technical Intricacies

Most kicks have strategic importance. Their object is not just to hurt the opponent, but to also act as a possible diversion. This means that athletes kick low, in order to force their opponent to lower his defenses, so that they can launch an attack by striking with their hands or proceeding with a body hold.

# THE FRONT KICK

Figure 3.1. Bronze statue of Roman pankration athlete from Autun. During the Roman Empire, athletes belonged to professional clubs whose purpose was to promote their commercial interests. This is the period of specialization of the athlete and the technique of the game. Louvre Museum, Paris. (Drawing based on a photograph from the museum.)

## ANALYSIS

In figure 3.1 a Roman pankration athlete launches a front kick attack. Judging by the position of his body we can assume that he is ready to proceed with hand blows or is executing at least one block, or both. The details as created by the sculptor show his knowledge of kinesiology and effectiveness. The knee at the time of impact is bent at a ten-degree angle. This provides maximum force for the kick. The toes are lifted up, allowing the soft part of the sole to strike. The base (right leg) of the athlete is bent, in order to provide maximum balance during the kicking process. The athlete's body is erect, facing his opponent. This enables him to maintain his balance after the kick, both for defensive purposes and in order to proceed with a follow-up attack. The distance between his legs is relatively short. This, combined with the erect position of his body, leads us to suggest that his kick may have had a defensive character, rather than an aggressive one. From the angle of the drawing, he appears to be striking with the ball of the foot; this is not actually the case, but the ball of the foot does appear in many other depictions.

## CONTEMPORARY APPLICATION

### Front Defensive Kick (Pankration)

The athletes face each other (A) and as one approaches from the right, the one on the left immediately lifts his front (left) leg, arming it (B).

At the time of impact, the leg of the defender is bent at the knee, ideally at a ten-degree angle, in order to obtain maximum power (C).

# DIRECT STOMP-KICK

Figure 3.2. The statue in figure 3.1, from another angle. (Drawing based on a photograph from the museum.)

## ANALYSIS

Observing the same presentation from another angle, the conclusions are different. The athlete from this angle seems to be performing a direct kick at the knee of his opponent, a "stomp-kick," intending to break it.* It is possible that he has used his left arm to defend himself against a blow from his opponent's arm and then has gone on to further his defense with this kick. The kick blow is dealt with the heel, while he is ready to proceed with a direct right punch blow.

---

*The term *stomp* refers to the type of strike (by the arm or leg) in which, at the time of impact with the target, the athlete's joint is bent (the elbow if it is a punch or the knee if it is a kick) and the strike is focused and executed in such as manner as to go *through* the target rather than impact the surface of the target, like an ax blade striking a piece of wood.

## Contemporary Application

Again the kick is defensive, as at the moment one contestant closes the distance, stepping forward to launch a punch blow, the defender counters to his opponent's knee with the sole of his foot, as he blocks the incoming punch (A–B).

He then steps firmly on the floor and counterattacks with a power punch (C).

# FRONT TRAMPLE-KICK

Figure 3.3. Attic amphora, sixth century BCE, Vienna Museum. (Drawing based on a photograph from the museum.)

## ANALYSIS

This is a trample-kick, used today in submission fighting as well (pankration). It provides additional confirmation that in pankration, kicking was led by strategy. The front leg is lifted up and cocks.* Then it is fired at the opponent's knee. Since this restricts the mobility of the opponent, the first athlete closes the distance safely; he is able to continue his attack with other means because his opponent is occupied with probable damage to his knee.

---

*In various kicks, cocking means folding the leg before it is launched for the kick. Cocking allows stronger and higher kicks, and in circular or hooking kicks it increases the speed of the strike. Occasionally, kicks are executed without cocking the leg so that the striker's intentions are not "telegraphed" in advance to his opponent.

## Contemporary Application

While ancient pankration athletes would have proceeded with a direct power punch before coming to body contact with their opponents, in contemporary contests of submission combat, the attack usually ends by going to a clinch after a trample-kick on the opponent's knee. For example, athletes of Brazilian jiu-jitsu usually continue by making body contact with their opponent in order to drive him to the ground.

The attacker cocks his front leg (B).

Next, he tramples on his opponent's knee, keeping a safe distance (C).

He ends up by infiltrating his opponent's defenses and clasping the body of his opponent (D).

# DEFENSIVE KICK

## ANALYSIS

This mosaic provides a lot of information regarding Roman era pankration, as it contains a plethora of presentations from all battle zones.

The athlete on the left in figure 3.5 seems to execute a defensive kick high on his opponent's leg or at the hip joint itself. It is a kick made with the lower part of the sole or more likely the actual heel, which serves to undermine his opponent's composure, causing him to leave his head uncovered. At the same time it prevents a possible attack.

Figure 3.4. Mosaic showing ancient wrestling ring. Roman era, Tusculum, Italy. (Drawing from *Monumenti ineditti pubblicati dall'Instituto di corrispondenze archeologica*, 1857–63.)

Figure 3.5. Magnified part of the mosaic.

## Contemporary Application

The main aim of defensive kicks is not to truly injure the opponent, but rather to prevent any offensive initiative on his part. The basic feature of this kind of kick is correct timing. Only then can it be used to effectively prevent an attack from an opponent and enable an athlete to proceed with his own counterattack.

The athletes face each other (A).

The athlete on the right attacks by trying to infiltrate his opponent's guard and attempting a rear punch blow. The athlete on the left prepares to defend (B).

Before he is able to complete his attack, the attacker is stopped by a defensive kick at his pelvis. At the same time, the defender has blocked the offensive arm of the attacker (C).

# LOW KICK TO THE KNEE

Figure 3.6. Greek presentation, sixth century BCE, Paestum Museum, Italy. This is clearly pammachon as the warriors are armed.

## ANALYSIS

The fighter on the right executes a kick-blow with his knee, perhaps using the higher part of his calf, to the inside part of his opponent's leg. Combined with the hold he has on his opponent's shoulders, it seems as if he is trying to sweep him to the ground. This representation infers that blows to the legs were within the main framework of the strategy used in both pankration and pammachon. Sadly, there is no other image in the archaeological record that would confirm this hypothesis; however, photographic evidence in our family archives does confirm that this type of attack was used in the folk wrestling prevalent during (Christian) Greek festivals in the nineteenth and early twentieth centuries.

## Contemporary Application

### Circular Low Kick and Backward Sweeping

In the game of pankration, the kick is directed to different points than in pammachon, where the main objective is to inflict injury to the knee joint of the opponent. In pankration such kicks have a more strategic connotation and are aimed a little above the knee, on the thigh, in order to induce the fellow competitor to lower his defensive block. Such blows inflict intense pain as well as injury to the sciatic nerve, which results in restricted mobility of the opponent during the fight. This is a very important kick in pankration, because:

1. It is powerful.
2. It does not cause the attacker to lose his balance.
3. It does not offer the opponent the option of grabbing the attacker's leg.
4. It does not demand flexibility.

In contrast to other fighting contests, in pankration it is not a normal procedure to exchange blow after blow continually with one's opponent, until the winner wears down the other. The pankration athlete strives to inflict the worst damage possible with the fewest blows, preserving his option to either clinch with his opponent, or to keep him at distance, while maintaining his balance. For this reason, high kicks such as those used in the Korean art of tae kwon do (high kicks with the body leaning off the centerline) are absolutely unsuitable for pankration. There is no indication of anything resembling a modern "side kick" in the archaeological record of pankration—as a consequence, should the reader see a side kick being demonstrated by a modern-day pankration instructor, he should immediately consider the instructor suspect.

The leg commences its course slightly bent (not cocked). At the time of impact, the pelvis turns slightly, increasing the power of the blow, while the point of impact with the target is the inside of the calf (B).

After the low kick ends on the thigh of the opponent, the attacker may continue with a leg sweep, throwing his opponent to the ground (C–E).

# FRONT KICK

Figure 3.7. Pammachon. Parthenon Marbles, 447 BCE, British Museum, London.

## ANALYSIS

This is an important representation of a martial arts move in which infiltration of the opponent's defenses is combined with a protective block and a front kick. The kick is directed low, using the ball of the foot with the toes turned upward. The defensive block with the palm is executed with an extended arm, in which the defensive move is supported by the entire body. The block is directed against a downward cut by the centaur, who is obviously holding a sword, and at the point of critical timing, i.e., before the centaur's hand begins its downward path. Simply perfect!

# FRONT POWER KICK

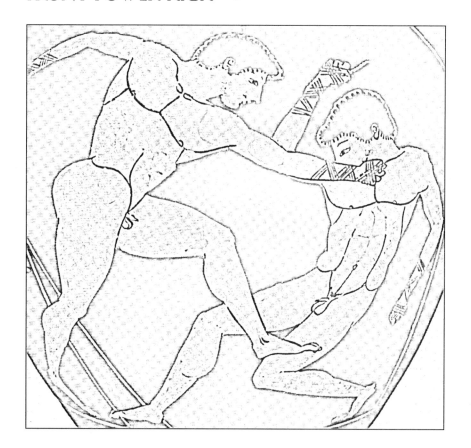

Figure 3.8. Pankration. Red amphora, early fifth century BCE, Athens, National Archaeological Museum. (Drawing based on a photograph from the museum.)

## ANALYSIS

This shows an attack by the athlete on the left with a "power" kick. The fact that this attack is being executed with the back leg is evident from the asymmetrical opposing postures of the athletes.

A power kick is executed with the back leg, with the aim of hurting the opponent. After impact, the leg steps down forward and does not return to its original position. This is what took place in the presentation shown (figure 3.8), where, after the kick, the defender resigned, indicated by his raised finger. During such a kick, the attacker drives through his target with the full strength of his body and full commitment of his will.

## Contemporary Application

"Power" kicks are executed with the rear leg and their intention is to generate the maximum of force while striking the opponent. This is readily achieved if the attacker targets the general area of his opponent's hips, so that during the kick his leg is perpendicular to the target, and if he keeps his knees slightly bent at the moment of impact. Once again, his focus should be on driving *through* the target.

The athlete on the left cocks his rear leg and drives it through the opponent's midsection (B–C).

After the kick, the attacker steps forward and is in position to continue his attack (D).

# JAMMING A KICK OR KNEE STRIKE

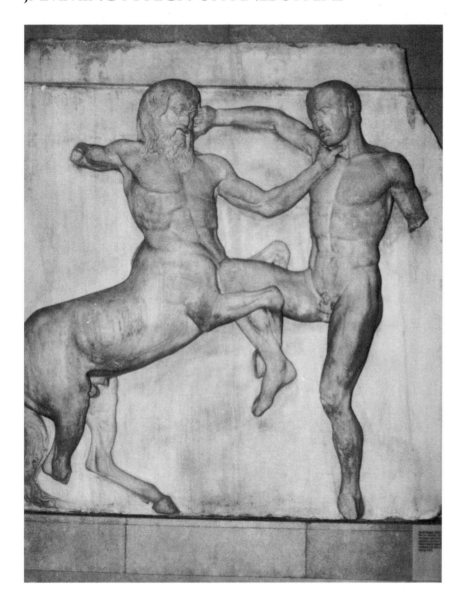

Figure 3.9. Pammachon. Parthenon Marbles, 447 BCE, British Museum, London.

## ANALYSIS

In this frieze from the Parthenon, both of the opponents have blocked their respective rival's attack against their genitals (or in the centaur's case, where the genitals would be if he were a man). At the same time, the Greek fighter deals a hooked punch to the temple of the centaur.

## CONTEMPORARY APPLICATION

### Jamming a Kick and Simultaneous Punch Attack

The athlete on the left, being under attack from his opponent, and defending against a possible punch blow (A) . . .

launches a hooking punch to his opponent's temple, while controlling his opponent's arm. At the same time he attempts a knee strike toward his opponent's genitals, which the opponent blocks with his leg (B).

# SEIZING A KICK

Figure 3.10.
Pankration.
Panathenean
Vase, 490 BCE,
Metropolitan Art
Museum, New
York. (Drawing
based on a photo
from the museum.)

## ANALYSIS

In this presentation, the athlete on the left has captured his opponent's leg while he was attempting a kick. The entire technique could be interpreted as per the sequence that follows.

## CONTEMPORARY APPLICATION

The athlete on the right prepares to attack his opponent with a kick (A–B).

The defender captures his attacker's leg (C).

With a suitable movement of his arms and his body, he causes his opponent to lose his balance and drops him to the ground, still holding his leg (D–E).

From this position he can easily apply a leg lock that will cause great pain and possible damage to the spine (we chose not to portray the technique because it is very dangerous).

## ANALYSIS

In this presentation of a bas-relief from the Temple of Apollo, a Lapith native has controlled the leg and arm of a centaur attacking with a sword. The breaking of the opponent's balance and his fall are based on the pendulum principle as shown in the contemporary application.

Figure 3.11. Pammachon. Bas-relief from the Temple of Epicurean Apollo in Vasses, fifth century BCE, British Museum, London.

## CONTEMPORARY APPLICATION

The athlete on the left attempts a kick, which is arrested by his opponent (A–B).

Trying to defend, he launches a punch blow, which his opponent blocks (C).

The athlete on the right then simultaneously seizes his opponent's arm, turns his body and jams his opponent's leg, throwing him forward (D).

He ends up with a leg lock (E).

ANALYSIS OF THE TECHNIQUES
OF PANKRATION

## Analysis of Movement in the Kicking Zone

At the time of executing a front kick there is a simultaneous explosive extension of the knee joint and a slight bend of the hip joint, with a contraction of the abdominal muscles. The angle of the thigh depends not only on the contractive force of the abdominal muscles, but—to a considerable degree—it depends also on how much the knee is bent and the consequential flexing of the rear thigh muscles. Therefore, correctly "cocking" the kicking leg is essential in order for the attacking athlete to achieve maximum power. The greatest part of the impact force of the frontal kick comes from the hip joint itself.

The following leg lifting exercises—meant for the abdominal muscles—can improve the power of the hip joint bend.

**Dynamic exercise:** Hanging from a bar, raise the legs up.
**Isometric exercise:** Raise the leg from a seated position, keeping the leg straight. Ankle weights can be used to increase the load.

When cocking the leg and firing the foot against a target, the pankration athlete must insure that the muscle groups used to bend the knee joint are well trained.

This can be accomplished by:

**Dynamic exercises:** Jumping exercises of all sorts and squats, made popular today by weight lifting, but utilizing lighter rather than heavier weights. If you are careful to avoid building excessive bulk, training with a partner of similar shape and size while doing a "fireman's carry" (i.e., carrying your partner on your shoulders) is also very good for enhancing the power of your kicks as well as adding strength to your "base."

During a kick, the attacking leg's movement is supported by the base leg through the extension of the hip joint, the knee joint, and the ankle. The aforementioned exercises will also help in building up the strength of the base leg during a kick, though striking an actual target is required to fully develop the coordination of base and striking legs.

# THE BOXING RANGE

## Principles and Aims

As pammachon evolved into boxing and pankration, the technique of delivering punches took different forms in the two games. In pankration punches were dealt from a greater distance than those in boxing contests. When pankration athletes came close to each other, they attempted to grapple with each other, which did not occur in boxing. As the fighters approached each other, a pankration athlete attempted to trap his opponent's limbs or clinch with him in order to initiate a throw or takedown and drive the fight to the ground. Our analysis of this combat range will make the differences between boxing and pankration explicit, as well as noting the reasons for the differences.

## Technical Intricacies

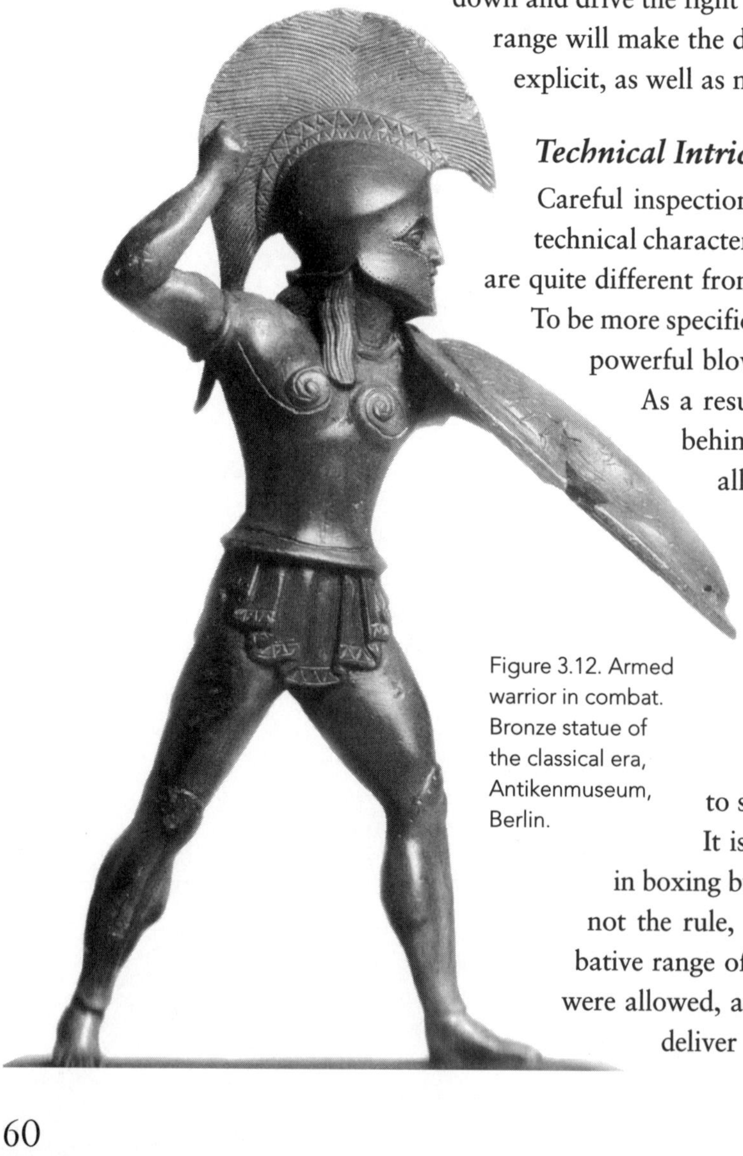

Careful inspection of various presentations reveals that the technical characteristics of a direct punch blow in pankration are quite different from the punches used in the game of boxing. To be more specific, pankration athletes sought to deliver one powerful blow instead of a sequence of multiple blows. As a result, they would "arm" their hand high up behind their head, with their elbow almost parallel to the ground! This move is derived from the battlefield: it is the move used to stab an enemy with a spear. The ancient preference for this elevated position is demonstrated by many representations in the archaeological archive, even in depictions of knife fights against an animal or in a duel, where one might expect to see a lower stance or upward thrust.

It is possible that the same principle was used in boxing but in specific instances only. It was certainly not the rule, because in the game of boxing, the combative range of engagement was fixed, only punch blows were allowed, and the aim of the contest was different: to deliver many continuous blows to the opponent,

Figure 3.12. Armed warrior in combat. Bronze statue of the classical era, Antikenmuseum, Berlin.

Figures 3.13 and 3.14. Drawings from Mycenaean seals showing scenes of combat; one shows a fight between a man and an animal, the other a duel between men.

who, according to the rules, could not use a clinch or any other method of avoiding or defending against blows except blocking with his arms. In the game of boxing, punches needed to be delivered quickly, while the athletes maintained their own defenses, and so their hands were placed closer to their bodies and heads; thus this more "closed-in" position became established for the sport, providing greater protection. The aforementioned position thus relates specifically to the intricacies of the game of boxing.

The ancient depictions of boxing show that the types of blows varied. We can see direct blows from a long distance, as in pankration, as well as direct punches from a shorter distance, with the hands in a defensive block near the head. In the close-up combat ranges—where pankration athletes would engage in trapping or wrestling—boxers used hooked blows from all angles in every way, as contemporary boxers do. So in the archaeological record we find hooked punches to the side of the head, uppercut punches to the chin, as well as hooked punches to the body. In the game of pankration, hooked punches were not used, at least not when the fighters were standing up. They were used only in ground fighting, primarily to wear down an opponent and weaken his defenses.

Figure 3.15. Boxing. Panathenean pot, 336 BCE, British Museum, London.

## ANALYSIS

### Front Punch (Jab)

This is a direct punch blow dealt with the front hand. The athlete on the right delivers a frontal blow with his left arm, leaning slightly backward, thus avoiding the rear punch blow launched by his opponent. This is a direct punch, the same as done today in contemporary "Western" boxing. The rear foot of the athlete is not fully on the ground; the heel is in the air, which offers him the option of swift moves.

### Rear Punch

This is a direct punch delivered with the rear hand. The athlete on the left attempts an attack using a rear punch blow, also used in contemporary boxing. The ancient artist has depicted remarkable details on the pot:

1. The turn in the shoulder area, which supports the offensive arm.
2. The turn in the pelvic area, which derives additional power from the pelvis.
3. The turn of the rear leg, which is raised on its toes in order to assist the entire effort to derive maximum power for this blow.

## CONTEMPORARY APPLICATION

This combination of a front and rear punch is done the same way in today's practice as in the ancient representation (A–B).

The turn of the body and the leg, done in order to derive maximum power, are characteristic of the rear punch (C).

# DIRECT POWER PUNCH

Figure 3.16. Pankration. Panathenean amphora, sixth century BCE, Louvre Museum, Paris.

## ANALYSIS

Figure 3.16 shows a direct power punch blow by the athlete on the left. The complete turn of the shoulder zone, combined with the arming of the right hand near and behind the head, preparing to launch a second blow, provide the impression of the power of such a punch. This punch has special significance in the game of pankration, different from the game of boxing. As mentioned earlier, in pankration punches were exchanged from a greater distance than in boxing, using the same kinesiology as that of fighters armed with spears. Today we can see the same type of punch blow used in no-holds-barred matches because it is more powerful. It is also used in some contemporary martial arts that emphasize self-defense.

In figure 3.17 the fighter on the left executes an "extended-knuckles" direct power punch with his left hand while arming his right hand, in order to follow up with the same type of punch blow. Here we can see the use of this type of punch in self-defense, since the vase drawing depicts close-quarter combat.

## Contemporary Application

The attacker paces forward, at the same time arming his hand at head level (A–B).

Taking a step forward he launches a punch, and turning his shoulder into the strike, he achieves maximum power (C).

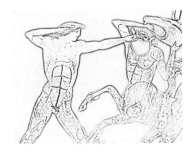

Figure 3.17. Pammachon. Direct power punch using an extended-knuckles fist. Florence Archaeological Museum, Florence, Italy. (Sketch based on a museum photo.)

Figure 3.18. Boxing. Attic amphora, 540 BCE, British Museum, London. (Drawing based on a photograph from the museum.)

# GUARD AGAINST DIRECT PUNCH BLOWS

## ANALYSIS

In figure 3.18 the athlete on the right is using the so-called passive guard, a defensive reaction seen mainly in boxing, when an athlete cannot avoid his opponent's punches and so protects his head in this manner. This is a useful method of defense, but it does not offer any chances for counterattack.

## CONTEMPORARY APPLICATION

In this contemporary application, the defender attempts to turn toward his rear leg while receiving a blow from his opponent, which gives him a chance to counter with his back hand, since it has in that way already been "armed."

# SIDE HOOK PUNCH
# AND FOREARM BLOCK

Figure 3.19. Boxing. Black-figure amphora, Louvre Museum, Paris.

## ANALYSIS

This is a very interesting representation, depicting another defensive block used in contemporary boxing. The athlete on the left executes a hooking punch to the side of his opponent's head, on the right. At the same time, he has armed his right hand, ready to launch a direct power punch. The athlete on the right is using the typical defense against a hooked punch, known as a "forearm block," because the blow lands on the forearm (in this case it is in fact the elbow), which is bent near the head.

## CONTEMPORARY APPLICATION

Forearm defensive block is followed by a counter and a hooked uppercut blow on the chin. During the time of impact, the defender turns his body and absorbs the blow with his forearm (A–B).

This is the ideal moment for the counter attack, since he is already at the right distance, and has already armed his left hand accordingly (C–D).

# HOOKED PUNCHES WHILE GRAPPLING ⟶

Figure 3.20. Greek statue, third century BCE, Galleria Uffizi, Florence. (Drawing based on a photograph from the museum.)

## ANALYSIS

As mentioned earlier, hooked punches are used in ground-fighting during pankration. In figure 3.20 the two pankration athletes are fighting on the ground. The athlete on the left tries to hit his opponent with a hooked punch. In order to protect his face the other athlete turns it the other direction, thus increasing the distance between him and his opponent. This would seem to indicate that punches to the back of the head (rabbit punches) were forbidden.

# HORIZONTAL HOOKING PUNCH

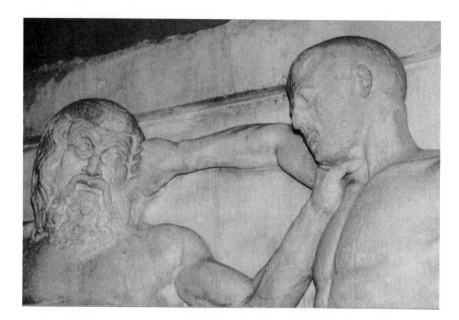

Figure 3.21. Pammachon. Parthenon Marbles, 447 BCE, British Museum, London.

## ANALYSIS

We examine this sculpture of the Greek fighter and the centaur once more in order to have a close-up view of the execution of the horizontal hooked punch on an anatomically vital point, used as a defensive measure in pammachon. This is an important representation of the many details of this technique. The man on the right uses a hooking punch to the side of the head with extended knuckles, with the intention of injuring his enemy-opponent, as he is at a disadvantage, his opponent having a hold on his neck. It is also a characteristic feature that he has placed his arm horizontally in order to further add power to his blow.

# FORWARD HOOKING PUNCH

Figure 3.22. Boxing or Pammachon. Amphora, 530 BCE, Museum Villa Giulia, Mingazzini. (Drawing based on photograph by M. Poliakoff from his book *Combat Sports in the Ancient World,* page 86.)

## ANALYSIS

This is a blow to the groin. However, no judge is present. It is a hooking punch blow; the elbow is bent at an angle in order to derive maximum power. Observe also how the aggressor has captured his opponent's wrist. The position of the attacker's body is worth noting. The athlete lowers his body in order to enhance his blow to the abdominal region. This type of body mechanics is used in modern boxing's "uppercut," whose target is the stomach rather than the groin. (In an actual fight, though, it is more effectively used when attacking the groin!)

## Contemporary Application

The contemporary application of a side hook punch shown above (A) could end up in a hooked punch blow to the body (B).

ANALYSIS OF THE TECHNIQUES
OF PANKRATION

# HOOKED PUNCHES

Figure 3.23. Pammachon.
Vase from Agia Triada, 1550 BCE,
Archaeological Museum,
Herakleion, Crete.

## ANALYSIS

This important presentation offers a plethora of information. The piece consists of four horizontal zones.

### First Zone

In the topmost zone there are two pairs of fighters. On the left the two fighters are shown face-to-face, exchanging hooking punches. The fighter on the right strikes his opponent with a "hooking body punch," while his opponent responds with a hooked punch to the side of his head. The pair of fighters on the right are practicing upward hooked punches. The metallic armor shown on the forearms of the fighters indicates this is pammachon, a simulation of armed combat, in which the metallic bars simulate a blade; it is not an athletic contest, but rather a ritual duel, the emulation of combat. Furthermore, it is obvious that the duel follows the same ritual as the stick fights depicted at the tombs in Beni Hasan and Thebes, Egypt, dating from 2000 BCE (c.f. figure 1.4), more than likely to the first blood.

### Second Zone

This is a scene from "bull fighting" (or, more accurately, "bull dodging"). This famous image, a somersault over a charging bull, holding its horns as a support base, has become world renowned and is indeed an exciting show of bravery.

### Third Zone

This representation has various interpretations. It is certainly not the classic punch blow of karate (*gyaku tsuki*), but more likely a downward punch made with the left hand of the fighter. This means that the hand was armed high and behind the head, exactly as in the direct power punch. The other hand is cocked at waist level, ready to attack. Thus it depicts a combination of blows, or, more likely, concerns a kind of defensive block with the left hand and stabbing attack to the abdominal area with the other hand, a natural outcome in the combat with a knife that is replicated in this ritual duel.

Figure 3.24. Gladiators. Roman lamp, first century CE, Römisch Germanisches Museum, Köln.

A Roman lamp of the first century CE shows a similar position in a duel between two armed men (figure 3.24). It suggests that the karate punch popular today is the natural evolution of the same move: a direct stab with a knife.

### Fourth Zone

The fourth zone of the Agia Triada piece shows the same technique as the third zone, as well as a possible throw and a backward breakfall, known in judo as *ushiro ukemi*.

# EXTERNAL BLOCK

Figure 3.25. Boxing. "Wine cup," 550 BCE, Cleveland Art Museum. (Sketch based on a museum photo.)

## ANALYSIS

The athlete on the right attempts a hooked punch to the side of his opponent's head. The athlete on the left responds by applying a "middle external block," a defensive blocking of the opponent's blow from the inside outward. He is preparing a counterattack with a direct power punch. This is a defensive block not frequently seen in contemporary boxing but found in the Eastern martial arts. It is called *seiken chudan uchi uke* in karate.

# EDGE OF HAND ("AX") STRIKE

Figure 3.26. Pankration. Panathenean amphora, sixth century BCE, Hermitage Museum. (Sketch based on a museum photo.)

## ANALYSIS

This is more likely pankration than boxing, because the athletes do not have their hands bandaged. We see a blow coming from the athlete on the left with the side of his palm. The arm is ideally bent at the elbow joint at the time of impact. He is preparing to pursue the attack with a direct power punch using the other hand. The athlete on the right seems to be taken by surprise and fails to block his opponent's blow, but he is preparing to counter with an upward hooked punch with his right. The correct position is characteristic for both athletes, as they turn their shoulders in opposite directions, enhancing their blows or their blocks. The edge of hand strike is characteristic in karate and is called *shuto uchi*.

## Contemporary Application

**Vertical Block and "Ax" Strike (Pammachon)**
The athlete on the right, using the defending arm, counterattacks with an outside "cut" with the edge of his palm to the neck (A–C).

This is a dangerous technique, banned in all contemporary combat sports. Pammachon!

# DEFENSIVE BLOCK WITH SIMULTANEOUS COUNTERATTACK AND HAMMER PUNCH

Figure 3.27. Boxing. Roman lamp, second century CE, Römisch Germanisches Museum, Köln.

## ANALYSIS

This is an important representation of a boxing game, with technical characteristics resembling Eastern martial arts. Specifically, the athlete on the left executes a rear punch, turning his body and leg characteristically. The athlete on the right reacts by deflecting his opponent's punch inward with his front hand. This is the same defensive block with the inside of the forearm that is used by Thai boxing athletes, as well as other boxers. The athlete stands on his toes, and he turns in order to block his opponent with the full power of his body, as well as to arm his other hand for a counter punch.

The punch blow that will follow from the athlete on the right is a downward hammer punch, a blow made with the soft base of the closed fist. The hand that executes the blow has been armed high above the head, in order to penetrate through the defensive guard of his opponent, in front of his head. This is a characteristic demonstration of the aim of the athletes of pankration—at least before the fourth century BCE—to "finish off" their opponents before having to go to the ground. This mentality shows the warlike, rather than sporting, orientation of ancient athletes. This exhibit comes from the Roman empire in any case, during a time when athletics in general and combat sports in particular had become completely specialized, because of the professional status of the athletes.

The same technique can be seen in karate, in various forms *(kata)*, though it is thought to be a double block and not a front hand block with concurrent arming of the other hand for counterattack. This blow is also often seen in no-holds-barred fights today, especially when the athletes are on the ground, because it has been established that it does not incur injury to the attacking athlete's hand.

## CONTEMPORARY APPLICATION

### Forearm Block and Hammer Punch

The opponent on the right attacks with a rear punch (A–B).

The defender reacts with a forearm block with his front arm, and at the same time arms his other hand to counterattack (B).

He completes his counterattack with a downward hammer blow to the head of his opponent (C).

# LUNGE AND MIDDLE
# HORIZONTAL DEFLECTION

Figure 3.28. Pankration or
Pammachon. Bronze Hellenistic
statue, first century CE,
British Museum, London.
(Photo copyright Kostas Dervenis,
1995. The use of this photograph
in any other publication, except
the magazine *Inside Kung Fu*,
which first published it, constitutes
unauthorized reproduction
without the permission of the
photographer.)

## ANALYSIS

This punch is used to penetrate an opponent's defense. This is why it is delivered with a fist in a straight line with the forearm. In this representation, the
athlete enhances the blow with a lunge covering the distance between himself and his opponent. We can observe that a "middle horizontal deflection"
takes place concurrently with the lunge, presumably because of a low shot
by his opponent, which he deflects to complete his own blow. The middle
horizontal deviation in karate is called *chudan soto uke*.

## CONTEMPORARY APPLICATION

### (Pammachon)

The attacker closes the distance step by step (A–B). Next, after deflecting his opponent's front punch, he proceeds with a right shot to the face, penetrating his opponent's defenses (C).

### Analysis of Movement in the Boxing Range

The different kinesiology demonstrated by the Hellenistic statue in figure 3.28 and the boxer on the Roman lamp in figure 3.29 offer some helpful distinctions regarding moves in the Boxing Range. They illustrate a difference in style between Greeks and Romans. In the oil lamp, from the Roman-German museum in Köln, the Roman boxer executes a punch blow, which very clearly resembles the *oi tsuki* of contemporary Japanese karate, a move that can be seen around the world today.

The statue in figure 3.28, on the other hand, shows the technique of delivering a powerful blow from a distance. As noted earlier, this reflects the ancient Greeks' adoption of the spear as their main weapon (**see** figure 3.12). Hence, their method of attack in combat resembled a "dance," as the fighter moved in and out of range of contact with his opponent, aiming at delivering a quick stab (or multiple stabs) with his spear. This suggests that the style of the pammachon and pankration of the Greeks was flowing and mobile—dancelike—as seen in the depiction of a Pyrrhic dance in figure 3.30, rather than static and powerful.

The Roman pankration athletes—seen in figures 3.1, 3.27, and 3.29—on the other hand, used a move that could be characterized as more static and powerful, resembling the classical karate of Okinawa and Japan. This kinesiology was developed by armored swordsmen who counted on a swift and dynamic defensive guard with a stable stance, in order to penetrate an opponent's guard and deal a severe blow with a short sword. The arm position at waist level in figure 3.29 is the same as that used by a warrior attempting to deliver a knife or sword blow to the opponent's abdomen.

In other words, in both the Greek and Roman methods, the requirements of armed combat were reflected in unarmed combat. Eastern karate was developed under similar conditions and needs. For example, many moves from Okinawan karate can be explained based on the use of the weapons *tonfa* (side-handle baton) and *sai* (pronged truncheon).

In figures 3.31 and 3.32 we see some more representations that clearly show the contribution of the stabbing move with a spear to the power punch blow in ancient boxing. When a power punch blow is dealt with the back hand (the more distant hand) the entire muscle system of the body participates. It seems logical that this type of punch blow was developed by fighters who used the spear as their main weapon.

The origins and development of the game of boxing are also demonstrated by other ancient presentations. The famous fresco from archaic

Figure 3.29. Roman lamp, first century CE, Römisch Germanisches Museum, Köln.

Figure 3.30. Pyrrhic dance. From a goblet, fifth century BCE. (Drawing based on photograph by Leonard Von Matt.)

Figure 3.31. Boxing. Black-figure amphora, British Museum, London.

Figure 3.32. Boxing. Red-figure amphora, British Museum, London.

ANALYSIS OF THE TECHNIQUES
OF PANKRATION

Figure 3.33. "Boxers." Wall drawing from the Thera cape, approximately 1500 BCE, National Archaeological Museum, Athens.

Santorini that shows two children boxing, shown in figure 3.33, is worth mentioning for many reasons. First, it is obvious that the boxer on the left is simultaneously executing a block and a blow with the same hand, a very advanced technique. Second, each boxer has only one of his hands bandaged. This could imply some kind of a ritual, possibly symbolizing the use of a weapon, in which case the gloves would have been reinforced, like the later-era Roman iron fist known as a *cestus*.

The use of the symbolic weaponry (helmets and forearm armor) seen in the depiction from the Agia Triada vase (figure 3.23) is paralleled in a similar ritual, which may also be very old, that is preserved today in India in the practice of *vajramushti*.* There, fighters wrestle and box while on one hand they wear a "thunderbolt," an iron fist with pointed ends on it. In Egypt, the same ritual duel to first blood appeared in 2000 BCE, with sticks. Most likely, all of the above had derived from religious rites during the Neolithic Era, as we shall see in chapter 4.

In figure 3.34, we see a boxing contest or pankration where the attacker on the left delivers a blow with his left hand, with the base of

Figure 3.34. Boxing or Pankration. Black-figure amphora, Olympia Museum.

---

*The first concrete historical testimonies about *vajramushti* originate in the fifteenth century CE, but the supporters of the theory that it has an Indian origin place its first appearance in 1000 BCE, an assertion that is backed up by its similarity to the 2000 BCE Egyptian stick fights.

ANALYSIS OF THE TECHNIQUES OF PANKRATION

his palm, while he is preparing to hit his opponent's neck with the side of his right hand. His opponent blocks with his forearm, preparing to react to the oncoming attack with an upward hooked punch.

Of course the evolution of boxing was not restricted to close punches or blows with the side of the palm. In figure 3.35, we see a boxing contest where both fighters have extended their thumbs, a very dangerous technique, which is aimed at injuring the eyes and the soft parts at the throat of the opponent. In the actual combat shown in figure 3.36, a Lapith villager is defending himself against a centaur, hitting him with an extended thumb on the ribs and spleen.

Figure 3.35. Boxing. Euboic amphora, sixth century BCE, Vatican Museum. (Drawing based on a museum photo.)

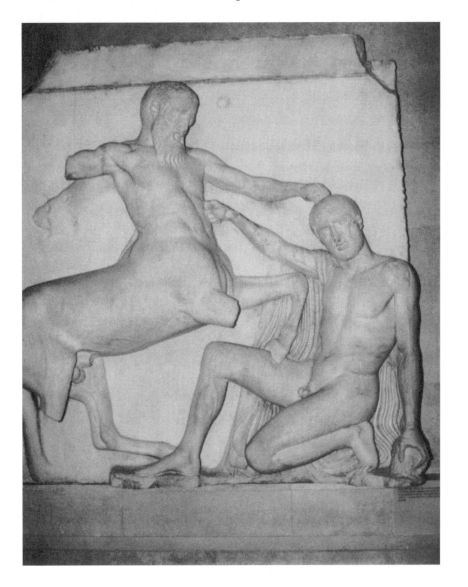

Figure 3.36. Pammachon. Parthenon Marbles, 447 BCE, British Museum, London.

Figure 3.37. Pammachon. Bas-relief from the Temple of Epicurean Apollo in Bassai, fifth century BCE, British Museum, London.

The use of punches with one or all the fingers extended was widely applied in ancient pammachon, less so in pankration, due to its dangerous potential. In figure 3.37, a depiction of an Amazon fight from the temple of Apollo in Bassai, the Amazon is defending herself by pushing her fingers into the armpit of her opponent, damaging his nervous and lymphatic systems. This move denotes deep knowledge of anatomy and martial arts. We can see a contemporary application in (A), where the attacker is on his toes from the pain, and the defender is preparing to throw him forward.

A famous use of an extended finger strike is recorded in the story of how Kreugas killed Damoxenos in pankration by breaking his ribs and penetrating his thorax with his fingers. It seems as if the use of fingers was a forbidden practice in pankration because Kreugas was expelled from Olympia for his action, that is, for using a pammachon battle technique in the athletic contest of pankration.

Above left: Figure 3.38. Statue of Damoxenos. Damoxenos has lifted his arm in order to meet his opponent's punch, a fatal error. Neoclassic work by Canova, 1802, Vatican Museum.

Above right: Figure 3.39. Statue of Kreugas. Neoclassic work by Canova, 1802, Vatican Museum.

ANALYSIS OF THE TECHNIQUES
OF PANKRATION

# Wrestling

It is not clear whether the game of wrestling in ancient Greece had the same rules as the modern game of submission wrestling because there is no clear information concerning ground wrestling. We do know that the main goal of the game of wrestling was to throw one's opponent to the ground, and not necessarily to achieve the submission of one's opponent. In Egypt, on the other hand, the aim was clearly the surrender of the opponent, as attested to by the frescoes at Beni Hasan, the "Bible of submission wrestling." They include a plethora of depictions of techniques such as submission holds and locks on the ground. We can safely state that all of the fundamental techniques of contemporary submission wrestling are depicted in these presentations from ancient Egypt.

It is interesting to note that in submission wrestling there is an absence of holds in the hand and elbow areas. This is logical and demonstrates that it is a combat sport and not a martial art. Entrapments—holds of the hand and elbow of the opponent—are characteristic of armed combat or unarmed combat with the possible presence of a concealed weapon. These holds are executed in order to control and disarm an opponent, especially in case he carries a close-quarter weapon (such as a knife or a club). However, in the battle for submission—in pankration for example—athletes do not attempt disarming techniques; this is why such images are distinctly pammachon.

# THE ENTRAPMENT RANGE
# AND THE WRESTLING RANGE

## Principles and Aims

In the combat sport of submission wrestling, which is divided into erect wrestling and wrestling on the ground, the fight naturally flows from the Entrapment Range to the Wrestling Range. In effect, the Entrapment Range is the beginning of the transfer of the fight to the ground. A variety of techniques are used in the Entrapment Range, blows as well as wrestling. It is perhaps the most unclear battle range, as well as the most difficult for the athletes since, among other difficulties, there is the threat of clinching and being thrown to the ground. In any case, the main characteristic of this zone is the pulling and pushing of limbs, as well as some kind of control.

## Technical Intricacies

The techniques of the Wrestling Range coincide with those of the Entrapment Range. The main characteristics of both ranges are limb entrapments, throws, and immobilizing the opponent with controls and finishing locks.

In the Entrapment Range, the main characteristic is the holding and engulfing of the head, an upper limb, or the body of one's opponent. The most frequent goal is to throw the opponent to the ground and continue the fight there, obtaining an advantageous position. Certain blows are included in this framework, with the aim of loosening the opponent's defenses, in order to place a hold on him. In ancient practice such blows were dealt with the knees, the elbows, or even with the head, according to recorded evidence. It is almost certain that such blows were not exchanged in order to finish off the opponent, but were used to inflict pain, possibly to cause him to lose his balance and to reduce the capacity of his defenses.

# KNEE BLOWS

Figure 3.40. Pankration. Roman athletes, second to third centuries CE, Vatican Museum. (Drawing based on photograph by Michael Poliakoff.)

## ANALYSIS

An important and revealing image. The athlete on the right—reacting to a front punch blow by his opponent—initially executes what is known in boxing as a "weave": he leans his head out of the range of the blow. At the same time, he grabs his opponent's arm and proceeds with a counterattack, delivering a blow with his right hand and a vertical knee strike to his opponent's groin. This is a magnificent combination of a defensive block, avoidance, blows, and correct timing, which characterizes athletes of a very high standard. Unsurprisingly, the depiction dates from the era of specialization and professional athletes and gladiators.

## CONTEMPORARY APPLICATION

In order to deliver a powerful blow with the knee, the attacker must hold one of his opponent's limbs to prevent defensive reactions. This could be the head, ideally, or an arm. Knee blows to the body must be executed vertically to the front rather than the side of the body, as this would offer the opponent the possibility of capturing the leg of the attacker.

The athletes are in the entrapment zone. The athlete on the left has ideal control of his opponent, holding his arm and head (A).

Powerfully pulling his opponent's arm and head, he delivers a knee blow (B).

The knee blow to the head may also be delivered from farther away, while pulling the head with both hands (C).

# HORIZONTAL OUTSIDE ELBOW

Figure 3.41. Pammachon. Temple of Zeus pediment, Olympia Museum. (Drawing based on a photograph from the museum.)

Figure 3.42. Pankration. Part of a pot, fourth century BCE, Staatliche Museum, Berlin.

## ANALYSIS

In figure 3.41 the centaur has captured the Greek woman from behind and she reacts by executing a horizontal outside elbow strike, supporting her blow by turning her body into the strike.

In figure 3.42 we see an excellent presentation, which shows a very high standard of technique and knowledge. The athlete on the right has grabbed his opponent's throat. If such a hold is accompanied by movement from the waist, it could cause serious damage. The athlete on the left reacts initially by grabbing the arm of his opponent, mostly to restrict his mobility. At the same time he executes a front power kick and a horizontal outside elbow blow. The opponent bleeds, which shows the faultless execution of this action. Such use of knees and elbows is characteristic of contemporary Thai Boxing (*Muay Thai*).

## CONTEMPORARY APPLICATION

### Outside Elbow Blow with an Arm Hold

The first priority in response to a single hand neck grab (choke) is to restrict the mobility of the opponent's arm (A).

It is useful to restrict the mobility of his arm both at the wrist joint and at the elbow joint (B).

The defender then proceeds with an outside elbow blow, maintaining the hold on his attacker's arm. While this blow would not ensure the defender's safety, it would surprise and stun the attacker and offer the opportunity to continue a counterattack or attempt to disengage (C).

## ANALYSIS

In figure 3.43 we see that the athlete on the right has trapped his opponent's head and prepares to deliver a hammer fist with his other hand. It is worth noting that the defender—in order to save himself from choking—bites his opponent's arm. The judge intervenes on the penalty by striking the offending athlete with his stick.

Figure 3.43.
Pankration.
Panathenean
amphora,
British Museum.
(Drawing based on
photograph from
the museum.)

# ARM PULLS AND CONTROL

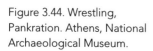

Figure 3.44. Wrestling, Pankration. Athens, National Archaeological Museum.

## ANALYSIS

In figure 3.44 the wrestlers are trying for arm control, while keeping a safe distance by forehead contact. In figure 3.45 Peleas's intention is evident: he is trying to pull Atalante's hand in order to achieve a rear body hold. Arm control is a basic point of concern, primarily in wrestling, but also in pankration, because a strong hold and pull of one or both arms results in successful positioning, offering a choice of techniques, mostly throws.

Figure 3.45. "Atalante against Peleas." Attic amphora, Antikensammlugen Museum, Munich.

# ARM PULLING AND REACTIONS

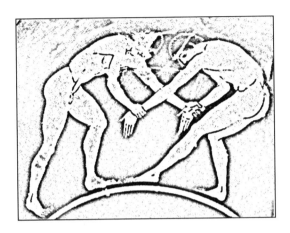

Figure 3.46. Attic cup, 480 BCE, Ashmolean Museum, Oxford. (Sketch based on photograph from the museum.)

## ANALYSIS

This depicts a scene from a gymnasium, where youth trained in wrestling. The athlete on the left has grabbed hold of both of his opponent's arms and pulls him. The athlete on the right reacts correctly, applying three important defensive options:

1. backward sliding, placing his hips at a distance,
2. forehead contact with his opponent, controlling and restricting his efforts to close in, and
3. inward turning of the palms, freeing his hands from the hold.

# TRANSPOSITION AND REAR BODY HOLD

Figure 3.47. Red-figure vase, 525 BCE, Staatliche Museum, Berlin.

## ANALYSIS

In figure 3.47 we see the transposition from an arm pull to a rear body hold. The athlete on the right has let go of his opponent's arm, which he had pulled, and tries to get behind him. However, the athlete on the left has grabbed hold of his opponent's left arm, obstructing the completion of his hold. At the same time, though, the attacker has caught his opponent's arm behind his back, enabling him to pull it and complete a body hold. The artist has provided tremendous detail and sequence of techniques and counter-techniques.

In figure 3.48, we see the final phase of an arm pull: a rear body hold executed by the athlete on the right. He has achieved close contact on his opponent; he has also lowered his pelvis perfectly, to set his base lower than that of his opponent, giving him the advantage of being able to lift him off the ground.

### Husking

Figure 3.48 also depicts the effort of the athlete on the left to disengage by attacking the top hand of his opponent. He passes his fingers under the right hand of his opponent while preparing to use his thumb on his left arm in order to open up the situation. This is called "husking" and is used today in submission wrestling.

Figure 3.48. Wrestling. Panathenean vase, 360 BCE, from Eretria, Eretria Museum.

ANALYSIS OF THE TECHNIQUES
OF PANKRATION

## Contemporary Application

### Arm Pulling and Transposition to Rear Body Hold and Husking (Submission Wrestling)

Arm pulling in the entrapment and wrestling zone is decisive because it makes it possible to transpose to a rear or side body hold on the opponent (A).

It is important to use the whole body in arm pulling and not just the strength of the arms (B–D).

At the close contact position the attacker presses his head into his opponent's back and lowers his pelvis below his opponent's (E).

The defender reacts by lifting his elbows high and placing his thumbs between his body and his opponent's upper arm (F).

After lowering his body suddenly, he pushes his opponent's arm off, pressing it with both hands (G).

ANALYSIS OF THE TECHNIQUES
OF PANKRATION

# HIP THROW

## ANALYSIS

In both depictions the wrestler on the right has grabbed his opponent's right arm and pulls him in preparation for a hip throw. At the same time he passes his right arm around the waist of his opponent, infiltrating his defenses. Next, he will turn inward and lower his hips in order to execute a hip throw, a move called *ogoshi* in judo and jujutsu.

Figure 3.49. Wrestling. Panathenean vase, 367 BCE British Museum, London. (Sketch based on photograph from the museum.)

## CONTEMPORARY APPLICATION

The athlete on the left opens his opponent's grip and passes his arm around his waist (A–B).

Figure 3.50. Wrestling. From tomb 15 at Beni Hasan, Egypt, 2000 BCE. (Drawing by P. E. Newberry, from the publication *Beni Hasan*, London, 1893.)

Turning inward and lowering his hips, he lifts his opponent up and throws him over his hip (C–D).

In submission wrestling, once one athlete is thrown to the ground, the attacker can either go to the ground also or can remain standing up and, ideally, entrap his opponent's arm, a pammachon move (E).

# BODY THROW

Figure 3.51. Wrestling, Pankration. The athlete on the left attempted a body hold, but his opponent on the right is using a body throw to overturn him. Attic vase, 520 BCE, Vatican Museum.

## ANALYSIS

Both depictions demonstrate a precise application of a body throw, what is known today in judo and jujutsu as *tai otoshi*. The athlete executing the throw pulls his opponent's hand, holding him with a headlock or controlling his body with his other arm. Next, he blocks his opponent's leg and turns his body abruptly.

Figure 3.52. Wrestling, Pankration. Bas-relief, first century CE, the Delphi Museum.

## CONTEMPORARY APPLICATION

The athlete on the right, passing his antagonist's defenses, grabs his opponent's head and places his left leg outside his opponent's distant leg (A–B).

The throw is executed with an abrupt turn of the body in the opposite direction (C–D).

He immobilizes his opponent on the ground with a hand lock and knee pressure on his head (E).

# MAIN OUTSIDE THROW

## ANALYSIS

The presentation of "Theseus against Kerkyon" in figure 3.53 is complex and demands detailed analysis. On the right, Kerkyon attempts the throw known as *osotonage* ("main outside throw") in jujutsu on Theseus. It is certain that Theseus is not attempting osotonage (or even *osotogari*, "outside reaping"), as his balance has already been broken, shown by the position of his body and the way he is leaning backward.

Figure 3.53. Attic red goblet, fifth century BCE, British Museum, London.

## CONTEMPORARY APPLICATION

First, let us examine osotonage, the throw Kerkyon is attempting.

The athlete on the right "opens" his opponent's guard, breaking his balance, outward (A–B).

Next, he attacks his opponent's thigh with his own, sweeping at his base, throwing him to the ground under control (C–D).

## ANALYSIS

In figure 3.53 Theseus, confronted by Kerkyon's osotonage, has two defenses to choose from. In the representation on the goblet, Kerkyon's right hand cannot be seen. If Kerkyon is armed (Theseus is shown carrying a sword on his back) with a knife in his right hand, Theseus must proceed immediately to execute an "outside throw reversal," known in Japanese judo as *osoto gaeshi.*

## Contemporary Application

### Outside Throw Reversal

The athlete on the left attempts osotogari (A).

His opponent on the right lowers his base, regaining his balance (his "center"), while breaking his opponent's balance (B).

Next, "launching" his body, the athlete on the right throws his opponent into the air and drops him to the ground, obtaining control of him (C–E).

## Analysis

Theseus's second option is to accept the throw and take advantage of its force to turn it against his opponent. Such a clever reaction would be worthy of the hero who is considered to be the creator of pankration. However, in order to execute this technique—known in Japanese as *yoko wakare*, "side flow"—it would be necessary for Kerkyon to be unarmed. It is our belief that the artist wanted to depict this situation, due to the way Theseus's hands are placed, holding Kerkyon.

## Contemporary Application

### Side Flow Technique

The athlete on the right attempts osotogari. The athlete on the left accepts the throw, capturing the body and arm of his opponent, and twisting on his legs in such a way as to deprive his opponent of the possibility of holding on to him (A–D).

ANALYSIS OF THE TECHNIQUES
OF PANKRATION

Next, this athlete throws his opponent over his body, holding his lower arm tightly; the outcome of this throw is a complex arm dislocation on the attacker's elbow as his opponent keeps holding him and proceeds to mount and subdue him (E–G).

# SHOULDER THROW

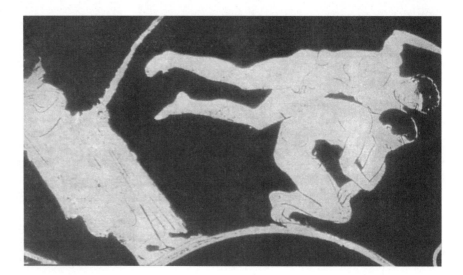

Figure 3.54. Wrestling, Pankration. Red-figure goblet, fifth century BCE, British Museum, London.

## ANALYSIS

This is a depiction of a shoulder throw done in the best way, known in judo and jujutsu as *seionage*. In contests such as submission wrestling or judo, after the throw, the athlete aims to continue on the ground, usually in a headlock. However, in actual self-defense, he would remain standing. In this presentation, the fact that the athlete does not kneel, as well as the fact that he is on his toes on both legs, probably denotes that he does not intend to follow his opponent to a ground fight but to remain standing.

## CONTEMPORARY APPLICATION

### Shoulder Throw (Wrestling, Pammachon)

The athlete on the left moves inward toward his opponent, making a 180-degree turn while holding his arm, and "loads" him on his back and shoulder (A–C).

Using his hip, he throws him over his body (D).

He finishes off by controlling his opponent's elbow joint (E).

Figure 3.55. Pammachon. Sculpture from the fifth century BCE, Olympia Museum.

## ANALYSIS

In this sculpture from the Temple of Zeus in Olympia, the centaur has escaped from the strangulation hold of the Greek by biting his lower arm, and holding his triceps and his hand. Next, he will attempt a shoulder throw.

## CONTEMPORARY APPLICATION

### Shoulder Throw (Pammachon)

The attacker attempts rear "naked" strangulation (so called in judo because the bare forearm is used), intending to take his opponent to the ground and finish him off (A).

The defender first breaks his opponent's balance as well as his hold, by turning his body and attacking his opponent's thigh at the same time (B).

Next, while the attacker tries to pull him back, he grabs his hand and attacks his triceps (C).

With explosive force, the defender throws his attacker forward with a shoulder throw and controls him intending to continue with ground fighting (D–E).

# "ARM-WRAPPING" THROW

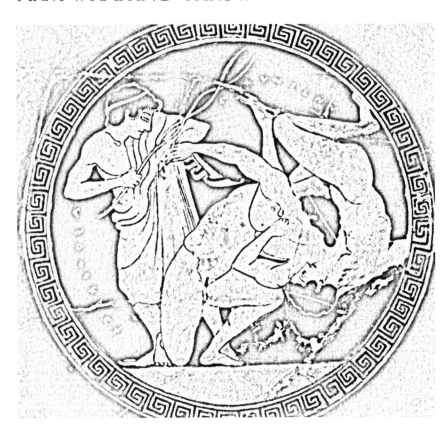

Figure 3.56. Wrestling. Attic cup, 500 BCE, National Library, Paris. (Drawing based on photograph from the museum.)

## ANALYSIS

This is an important representation of the variety of throwing techniques known to the ancients. It is not clear which type of throw it is. At first glance we would suggest that it is a final throw after a body lift on the shoulders, known in Japanese as *kata guruma*. It could also be a shoulder throw with a vertical body drop, known in judo terminology as *seoi otoshi*. However, the hand placement of the athletes is not in accordance with this technique. There is an unclear spot in the image on the cup where the face and perhaps the arm of the athlete attempting the throw would be seen. If it were a throw that included "wrapping up" the opponent's arm, then it would be similar to the judo technique *soto makikomi*. To maintain a variety of applications in the text, we specifically present the latter technique here.

## CONTEMPORARY APPLICATION

Reacting to an attempt at a headlock, the defender lowers his own head and escapes temporarily (A–B).

The defender continues and grabs his opponent's arm with both hands (C).

The defender continues to turn. Having placed his leg outside his opponent's legs, he sweeps him (D–E).

# REAPING HIP THROW

## ANALYSIS

This image constitutes one more interesting piece of information from ancient Egypt of 2000 BCE. The athlete on the right is pulling his opponent by the arm while making an inward turn; then, using his leg to "reap" his opponent's body, he can sweep him over that leg and throw him. In this case, the way he turns his body is a characteristic indicating he has applied correct technique, rather than trying to throw his opponent by brute force. This is a basic throwing technique known in contemporary judo as *harai goshi*.

Figure 3.57. Wrestling. From tomb 2 at Beni Hasan, Egypt, 2000 BCE. (Drawing by P. E. Newberry, from the publication *Beni Hasan*, London, 1893.)

## CONTEMPORARY APPLICATION

We shall examine two different contemporary applications of this technique. The second option will be presented on page 144 as one of contemporary applications of the "Heel 'Hooks' as Means to Throw and as Counters" exercises.

The athlete on the right penetrates his opponent's guard, controlling his head and arm. Next, he turns, placing his hip in front of his opponent's body (A–B).

With a dynamic movement, he sweeps his opponent's base, while pulling his head and arm simultaneously (C–D).

He finishes by trapping his opponent's hand under his arm, and controlling his elbow joint. He applies knee pressure on his opponent's head, restricting his mobility and his chance to turn (E).

# INSIDE THIGH SWEEP

Figure 3.58. Wrestling. From tomb 29 at Beni Hasan, Egypt, 2000 BCE. (Drawing by P. E. Newberry, from the publication *Beni Hasan*, London, 1893.)

## ANALYSIS

This throw is similar to the *uchimata* in modern judo, as shown in the contemporary application (A).

# OUTSIDE KNEE/CALF SWEEP

## ANALYSIS

This throw resembles the throw *hiza guruma* in modern judo. If it were pammachon, it would be executed as a kick instead of a sweep.

## CONTEMPORARY APPLICATION

The athlete on the right, after having broken his opponent's balance, controlling the upper part of his body (A–B), sweeps the knee area of his opponent with the sole of his foot (C), throwing him on the ground, where he controls him (D).

Figure 3.59. Pankration. Panathenean amphora, 480 BCE, Hood Art Museum, Dartmouth University, Hanover, New Hampshire. (Drawing based on photograph from the museum.)

# OUTSIDE FOOT/ANKLE SWEEP

Figure 3.60. From tomb 15 at Beni Hasan, Egypt, 2000 BCE. (Drawing by P. E. Newberry, from the publication *Beni Hasan*, London, 1893.)

## ANALYSIS

This throw resembles the move known as *de ashi harai* in contemporary judo. The athlete on the right (the dark figure) sweeps his opponent's ankle, after having already broken his balance, controlling the upper part of his body.

# ELBOW CONTROL

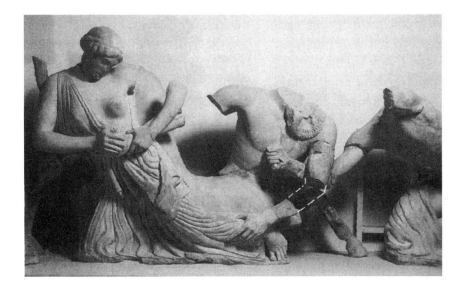

Figure 3.61. Pammachon. Part of the ornamentation of the temple of Zeus at Olympia, Olympia Museum.

## ANALYSIS

This is a control and disarming lock, which was well known to the ancients, but was used more in pammachon than in pankration. This is logical, because trapping the arms—when not followed by immediate execution of throws (a characteristic feature of combat sports)—denotes control and disarming of one's opponent. The defender, turning her body accordingly, traps the centaur's hand ideally, thus controlling his elbow and hand, neutralizing a possible attack with a hold or a stab with a close-quarter weapon (such as a knife). This is a joint "lock," an immobilization and attack on the joint, which will lead to a direct elbow dislocation if the pressure continues. At the same time, we see the counter technique to this application: the centaur grabs the woman's leg with his free hand. This hold, combined with lifting of the body, would neutralize the elbow hold and would cause the defender to fall to the ground, so, in the ornamental frieze, another Lapith villager intervenes and places a knife at the centaur's throat.

## CONTEMPORARY APPLICATION

### Elbow Control (Pammachon)

Such locks are very difficult to achieve in pankration, as an athlete's arm is unlikely to be exposed long enough to be trapped.* This type of move, however, can happen quite frequently during a real attack. During an actual fight, emotions run high and we rarely encounter two well-prepared athletes who are psychologically prepared to battle one another. At the same time, the commitment of all of one's efforts in a single attack, in an attempt to quickly penetrate the opponent's defenses and finish him, occurs quite frequently in conditions of actual fighting, armed or unarmed.

The attacker on the right holds the other one's throat and prepares to attack with a punch to the face (A).

The defender reacts by holding his opponent's arm and executing a backward turning step (B).

---

*In a ground fight, an athlete's arm can be exposed longer than in a standing fight. Also, on the ground, an athlete can trap his opponent's arm using the natural obstacle of the ground, which restricts his mobility.

At the same time he traps his opponent's elbow and hand (C).

But, as he presses his opponent's arm, the combatant on the right starts defending himself by grabbing his opponent's leg (D).

He raises his body and lifts the leg of the combatant on the left, disrupting the power of the elbow lock (E).

# LIMB LOCKS WITH DIRECT AND COMPLEX DISLOCATIONS

Figure 3.63. Pankration. Hellenistic bronze statue, Antikensammlungen Museum, Munich. (Drawing based on a photograph from the museum.)

Figure 3.62. Pankration. Hellenistic bronze statue, British Museum, London.

## ANALYSIS

In figure 3.62 we see that the athlete on the left has trapped one of his opponent's arms under his own arm and is holding his opponent's other arm by the hand, extended. At the same time, he has stepped in front of his opponent, intending to sweep and throw him to the ground. With his arms trapped, this fall would be painful, as he would land on his head.

In figure 3.63, the hold presented is similar to the one in figure 3.62. Here, too, the wrestler on the left has trapped one of his opponent's arms under his arm and holds the other one extended. At the same time, while standing behind him, he obstructs his opponent's efforts to escape by placing his leg in front of the other's. This shows a refined technique of immobilization, possible throwing, and even an application of a finishing hold (a hold designed to force the opponent to submit due to pain or pressure).

In figure 3.64, we have another excellent representation. This time, immobilization is not accompanied by arm trapping but by a leg hook. At the same time, the attacker has passed his opponent's outstretched arm in front of his waist, trapping it. With his other hand, he pushes his opponent's head downward. This technique shows that the ancients had profound knowledge concerning the principles and kinesiology of the human musculoskeletal system.

### Recapitulation

These three representations lead us to the following conclusions:

1. All three statues belong to the Hellenistic era. This means that athleticism had not yet become highly specialized. Athletes still fought in the wrestling ring in a way that was also applicable in actual battlefields, striving to finish off an opponent before having to go with him to a prolonged fight on the ground.
2. Although all three presentations depict athletic contests, control of the limbs is a technique used more in martial arts than in combat sports.
3. In addition to controlling the opponent, all three sculptures show situations where, should the pressure of the locks being applied persist, the opponent would suffer a limb dislocation, either with direct dislocation of the hyper-extended elbow joint or shoulder joint, in the case of the "straight" joint locks, or a complex dislocation of the shoulder and elbow joints, in the case of the secondary "bent" joint lock. Please note that in the first two depictions it is very simple for the wrestler on the left to snap the elbow joints with a dynamic movement utilizing the full force of his body.

Figure 3.64. Pankration. Egyptian bronze statue, Hellenistic era, British Museum, London.

## CONTEMPORARY APPLICATION

The attacker (on the left) places his arm inside his opponent's and twists, trying to hold his opponent's same side shoulder (A–B).

He lowers his arm, having trapped his opponent's bent arm (C–D).

He finishes by exercising pressure, holding his opponent's head and pushing it the other way, while restricting his opponent's mobility by countering with his knee (E).

# CIRCULAR SACRIFICIAL THROW

## ANALYSIS

This is the throw known in judo as *tomoenage*.

## CONTEMPORARY APPLICATION

The athlete on the left enters under the center of gravity of his opponent (A–B).

After placing one or both of his legs at the base of the pelvis of the other athlete (or between his legs), he abruptly stretches his legs with a vertical move, throwing his opponent above him (C).

He continues with a roll and mounts the opponent to finish him. Note the control of the opponent's arms with his body. (D).

Figure 3.65. From tomb 15 at Beni Hasan, Egypt, 2000 BCE. (Drawing by P. E. Newberry, from the publication *Beni Hasan*, London, 1893.)

# HEAD LOCKS

Figure 3.66. Wrestling. Theseus is wrestling with Kerkyon. Attic vase, 510 BCE, Museo di Antichita, Torino. (Drawing based on photograph from the museum.)

## ANALYSIS

In figure 3.66, the athlete on the left executes a hold on the neck of his opponent, trapping his arm at the same time. His intention is probably to force him to the ground by making a backward turn with his left leg, which would turn his opponent so that his back was to the ground. The closing of this hold is effected with the fingers; it is the so-called Maeandrian grip. After the throw, he may transition to ground fighting and proceed with a "strangulation using the opponent's arm." This is a basic technique in submission wrestling.

In figure 3.67, we have another presentation of a headlock performed while trapping the opponent's arm. The athlete on the ground has trapped the arm of his opponent and is trying to force him to the ground. His opponent is trying to escape, hitting at his ribs with hooked punches.

Figure 3.67. Attic pot, 500 BCE, Metropolitan Museum of Art, New York. (Drawing based on photograph from the museum.)

Figure 3.68. "Hercules vs. Antaeus." Attic red-figure vase, the Louvre Museum, Paris.

In figure 3.68, we have a show of advanced technique by Hercules. He has Antaeus in a headlock, while at the same time he has trapped Antaeus's arm between his legs, executing a perfect direct elbow dislocation.

## Contemporary Application

### Head Lock with Arm Trap Leading to Strangulation

The attacker controls his opponent on the ground with a headlock (A).

The defender manages to free his arm with a "pump move." The defender pushes his opponent's chin with his hand, trying to create added space in the hold, in which to maneuver. The attacker holds his arm below the elbow (B).

Ideally, the attacker pushes his opponent's arm in front of his neck. He then closes in with his head and his arms clasping his palms, pressing hard (C).

While it, in fact, requires some skill to effect a strangulation with this technique, in conditions of close-quarter combat, it is sometimes important to remove the opponent's arm from your centerline of attack. This technique is primarily designed for this purpose. In addition, it is possible to safely attack the cervical vertebrae while using a modified version of this technique in unarmed close-quarter combat.

# HEADLOCKS, THROWS, AND LEG HOLDS

   a          b          c          d          e

Figure 3.69a, b, c, d, e. From the tombs at Beni Hasan, Egypt, 2000 BCE. (Drawing by P. E. Newberry, from the publication *Beni Hasan*, London, 1893.)

## ANALYSIS

In submission wrestling, as depicted in the Beni Hasan images, the headlock is used mainly for two reasons:

1. As an entrapment leading to a throw.
2. As a reaction to a throw or a leg hold.

In figure 3.69a–d the athlete on the right is trying to execute a throw with a headlock and the athlete on the left reacts with a leg hold. In figure 3.69e we see one more headlock on the ground. In figure 3.70a and b attempts by an attacker have been blocked by holds on one or both of his legs; the reaction is a headlock. From these representations, we can deduce that when one contestant attacks the head, the defender reacts by holding his opponent's base, in order to neutralize the moves that would lead to a throw. Also, when one athlete attacks his opponent's base, mainly one leg, the correct reaction is a headlock, so that the defender could take the attacker to the ground with him after the throw. This high standard of detailed knowledge of the techniques of combat sport was indeed impressive in Egypt in 2000 BCE.

Figure 3.70a and b. From the tombs at Beni Hasan, Egypt, 2000 BCE. (Drawing by P. E. Newberry from the publication *Beni Hasan*, London, 1893.)

## CONTEMPORARY APPLICATIONS

### Headlock and Throw

The attacker has grabbed his opponent's arm high on the triceps and, entering, he executes a headlock with his other arm (A–B).

He places his hip in front of his opponent and throws him with a powerful twist of his body (C).

Throwing him to the ground, he follows him, pressing him down with his body (D–E).

He consolidates by controlling three points: his opponent's head is in a headlock; with the same hand he holds his opponent's shoulder; with his other hand he controls the triceps, keeping the opponent's hand trapped under his arm (F).

### Headlock and Leg Hold

The reaction of the athlete to the attempted throw in the archaeological document shown in figure 3.69 can be seen in photographs A–D.

### Headlock, Leg Hold, and Counter Throw

The athlete on the right has executed a headlock on his opponent, in a standing position (A).

The defender reacts with a side body hold and by holding his opponent's near leg from the inside (B–C).

Next, he lifts his opponent off the ground, holding him from the hip as well, and drops him to the ground, fighting for control from a side hold-down position (D–E).

Figure 3.71. From tomb 17 at Beni Hasan, Egypt, 2000 BCE. (Drawing by P. E. Newberry, from the publication *Beni Hasan*, London, 1893.)

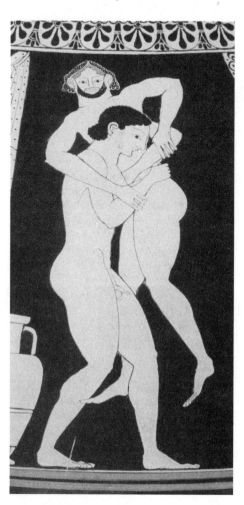

Figure 3.72. Attic red-figure amphora, Staatliche Museum, Berlin.

## ANALYSIS

Attacks on the opponent's body using body clinches (front, side, rear) were powerful tactics, mostly in wrestling contests (this technique is also called a "bear hug" in modern times). By executing such a hold against an opponent, the attacker would gain the advantage, because he could throw the opponent to the ground, often with devastating results. After a clinch, the main way to throw the opponent to the ground was either by lifting him up or by trapping his legs, with or without hooks. Both figures 3.71 and 3.72 depict a front body clinch and lift. In figure 3.72 the lifted athlete is attempting to free himself by "husking," a characteristic move in such cases.

# LIFT AND TURN TO THROW

Figure 3.74. From tomb 2 at Beni Hasan, Egypt 2000 BCE. (Drawing by P. E. Newberry, from the publication *Beni Hasan*, London, 1893.)

Figure 3.73. Attic cup, 530 BCE, Archaeological Museum, Florence. (Drawing based on a photograph from the museum.)

## ANALYSIS

In figure 3.73 the athlete on the left attacks, crossing his arms as he seizes his opponent's body, in the opposite orientation to a frontal body clinch. This is the correct hold for the technique described in classical texts as "raise him to the heights," which ends up with the opponent landing on the ground on his head.

Throws from body clinches may also take place by one athlete turning his opponent backward over his own body, as in contemporary wrestling today.

Figure 3.75. From the temple-tomb of Ramses B1 at Medinet Habu, Egypt, 1150 BCE. (Drawing based on a photograph from the University of Chicago, published in *Combat Sports in the Ancient World* by Michael Poliakoff.)

## CONTEMPORARY APPLICATION

**Lift to the Shoulders and Throw (Judo *kata guruma*, "fireman's carry")**

The attacker penetrates with his front leg between his opponent's legs (A–B).

Next, he ducks suddenly, bending his knees, and passes his arm as a hook between his opponent's legs (C).

He rises, having "loaded" his opponent onto his shoulders, and prepares to throw him to the side or to the rear (D).

# HEEL "HOOKS" AS MEANS
# TO THROW AND AS COUNTERS

a           b           c

Figure 3.76a, b, c. From tomb 15 at Beni Hasan, Egypt, 2000 BCE. (Drawings by P. E. Newberry from the publication *Beni Hasan*, London, 1893.)

## ANALYSIS

When wrestling in a standing position, heel "hooks" play a decisive role in controlling an opponent. They are used for two reasons:

1. As an obstacle, in order to drive the opponent to the ground, that is, as a means of attack (shown in figure 3.76).
2. As a defensive measure, in order to neutralize a possible lift or turn of the opponent's body, aiming to throw the defender to the ground (shown in figure 3.77 on page 138).

In figure 3.76a, we see the athlete on the left attacking his opponent's body, trying to force him to the ground by placing a hook on his front leg. In figure 3.76b, the athlete on the right has grabbed and is holding up the leg of his opponent, who reacts by holding the attacker's head. Next, aiming to drive his opponent to the ground, the athlete on the right places a hook on the base leg of the athlete on the left.

In figure 3.76c, the athlete on the right attacks his opponent's body with a front body clinch and tries to throw him by placing a hook on his front leg.

ANALYSIS OF THE TECHNIQUES
OF PANKRATION

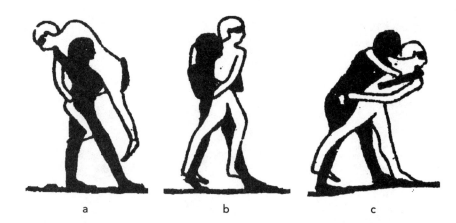

Figure 3.77a, b, c. From tomb 15 at Beni Hasan, Egypt, 2000 BCE. (Drawings by P. E. Newberry from the publication *Beni Hasan*, London, 1893.)

In figure 3.77a, the athlete on the left has caught his opponent between his legs with one arm, lifting him, and holding him with his other hand below his head. This is the technique known in contemporary judo as *kata guruma*. The athlete on the right reacts by placing a double hook with his calf on his opponent's thigh and his foot inside his opponent's knee joint. This way, he neutralizes the throw and can proceed with a choice of many counterattacking techniques.

In figure 3.77b, the athlete on the left attempts a lift following a rear body clinch. The athlete on the right reacts by placing double hooks on his opponent's legs. Next, in figure 3.77c, while his opponent lowers him down, he maintains the hook on the rear leg, at the same time grasping his opponent in a head lock. This will enable him to follow up with the "sweeping hip" throw *(harai goshi)* seen earlier.

## Contemporary Applications

### Hooks as Attack

The attacker passes his arms inside and executes a front body hold (A–C).

Next, he presses his head against his opponent's chest and places an outside hook on his opponent's front leg (D).

He sweeps the leg, while at the same time he squeezes him (E).

On the ground he secures a mounted position on his opponent's body, taking care not to be caught in half guard (F–G).

### Hooks as Counters

The attacker has executed a rear body clinch (A). He lifts his opponent off the ground (B). However the defender neutralizes the lift with a leg hook (C).

ANALYSIS OF THE TECHNIQUES
OF PANKRATION

**"Sweeping Hip" Throw** *(harai goshi)* **as a Reaction to a Wrestler's Lift**

This is the technique shown in figures 3.77b and c. The attacker has executed a rear body hold (A).

Against his opponent's attempt to lift him, the defender counters with a leg hook, neutralizing the attempt (B).

Next, as he steps down, he holds his opponent by the arm and the head (C).

As soon as he places his foot on the ground, he executes a body turn, pulling his opponent hard and sweeping at his base with his thigh. From then on, he will proceed to ground fighting from an advantageous position (D).

# LEG TAKEDOWNS

Figure 3.78a, b, c. From tomb
17 at Beni Hasan, Egypt, 2000
BCE. (Drawings by P. E. Newberry
from the publication *Beni Hasan*,
London, 1893.)

a          b          c

## ANALYSIS

Leg takedowns are very commonly used in submission wrestling and in free-style wrestling. This technique is almost always used when an athlete intends to follow his opponent to a ground fight, as the usual reaction to a leg takedown attempt is a reverse headlock choke (or "guillotine" as it is called in contemporary times; see page 144). Thus the athletes stay in close contact and the fight continues on the ground.

Figure 3.78 shows two different types of leg takedowns. In figures 3.78a and 3.78b both athletes on the left have bent down and use one or both hands to hold their opponents' legs near the knee joint, in order to lift them off the ground. In figure 3.78c the athlete on the left has already lifted his opponent's leg off the ground; he is holding one leg a little above the ankle with his right hand, and has passed his left arm around the thigh higher up. From this position, he can force his opponent to the ground in two ways, applicable today in submission wrestling:

1. With a linear move, entering and knocking the opponent off balance.
2. With a twisting move, taking a backward step and turning his body.

## CONTEMPORARY APPLICATION

The attacker grabs his opponent's front leg by the knee and holds it tightly to his chest, eliminating any openings his opponent might take advantage of (A–C).

Next, he enters the space between his opponent's legs and throws him to the ground (linear move) (D).

There, he immobilizes his opponent by trapping his other leg under his own leg. From this position he can proceed to a good number of attacking techniques for a ground fight (E).

# COUNTERS TO A FRONT LEG TAKEDOWN

The images presented in this section make it clear that, while attempting a front leg takedown, it is very important for the attacker to avoid leaving a gap between his opponent's leg and his own head. A gap allows the defender to proceed with counterattacking techniques such as a reverse forearm choke or neck crank.

## ANALYSIS

### Reversed Forearm Choke ("Guillotine") Counter to Front Leg Takedown

The ancient Egyptian image in figure 3.79 shows a reverse choke counter to a front leg takedown attempt. The athlete on the left had grabbed his opponent's leg and was attempting a throw. However, he left a gap, offering his opponent the chance to pass his forearm in front of his neck, which resulted in the choke represented in this image. The athlete on the right has also put his weight on his opponent's head, thus freeing his leg from his opponent's hold. The pair of athletes on the right in figure 3.79 demonstrate an attempted arm-bar throw and how to counter it.

Figure 3.79. From the temple-tomb of Ramses B1 at Medinet Habu, Egypt, 1150 BCE. (Drawing based on a photograph from the University of Chicago, published in *Combat Sports in the Ancient World* by Michael Poliakoff.)

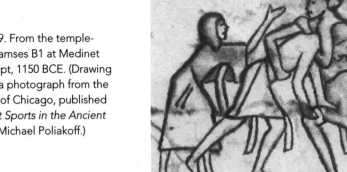

## Contemporary Application

If an attacker does not manage to close all the gaps
and keep his opponent's knee tight to his chest, then
he provides his opponent with the chance to place his
arm in front of his throat and execute a reversed choking or strangulation attack (A–C).

Figure 3.80. Theseus vs. Kerkyon. Attic cup, 460 BCE, Ferrara Archaeological Museum. (Drawing based on photograph from the museum.)

## ANALYSIS

### "Crucifix" or "Neck Crank" Counter to Front Leg Hold

The image in figure 3.80 depicts an instance in the mythological combat between Theseus and Kerkyon. Theseus has passed his forearms under the arms of Kerkyon, who is attempting a front leg takedown. Theseus is trapping his opponent's head under his armpit with under hooks. This is the perfect position from which to proceed with an attack on the joints of the cervical vertebrae (which can result in dislocation if applied with enough pressure). This move is called a "neck crank" or a "crucifix" in modern submission wrestling, the latter term due to the position of the opponent's arms when executing it.

Figure 3.81. "Crucifix" or "neck crank." From the tombs at Beni Hasan, Egypt, 2000 BCE. (Drawing by P. E. Newberry, from the publication *Beni Hasan*, London, 1893.)

ANALYSIS OF THE TECHNIQUES
OF PANKRATION

## CONTEMPORARY APPLICATION

The same—faulty—attack seen in the previous depiction (A).

This time the defender takes advantage of suitable gaps and passes his arms through them, placing them under his opponent's armpits (B).

He completes his counterattack by clasping his palms behind his opponent's, trapping his head under his armpit, applying pressure on his neck (C).

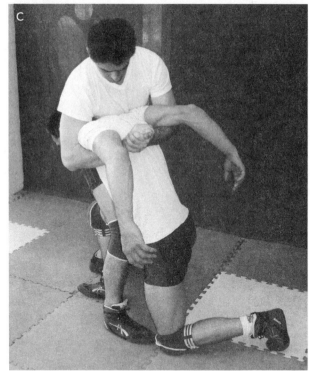

# DOUBLE-LEG TAKEDOWN

Figure 3.82. Wrestling. Attic amphora, fifth century BCE, Museo Nazionale, Tarquinia. (Drawing based on a photograph published in *Combat Sports in the Ancient World* by Michael Poliakoff.)

Figure 3.83. From tomb 17 at Beni Hasan, Egypt, 2000 BCE. (Drawing by P. E. Newberry, from the publication *Beni Hasan*, London, 1893.)

## ANALYSIS

In figure 3.82, we see an attempt to grab both legs. The athlete attacks without having previously bypassed his opponent's defenses by lowering his own body. Hence he is forced to duck, which offers his opponent the chance to grab him by the waist, with the clear intention of turning him over backward.

Conversely, in figure 3.83, we see that the attacker has lowered his own base adequately, not presenting his opponent the option of seizing him around the waist in a reverse grip.

Figure 3.84. From tomb 2 at Beni Hasan, Egypt, 2000 BCE. (Drawings by P. E. Newberry, from the publication *Beni Hasan*, London, 1893.)

In figure 3.84 we have two similar leg takedown attacks. In the representation on the left, the attacker pushes his head into his opponent's body, maintaining a distance, while he executes a takedown on both legs. In the representation on the right, the attacker places his head at his opponent's side, which, if not combined with a lowering of his base, allows the opponent counterattacking options, as in this case. The defender places his arms accordingly, preventing the other athlete from "penetrating," and keeping his opponent's pelvis and legs at a safe distance.

# "SPRAWL" (COUNTER TO ATTEMPTED DOUBLE-LEG TAKEDOWN)

Figure 3.85. Hercules vs. Antaeus. Attic amphora, 520 BCE, British Museum, London.

## ANALYSIS

In figure 3.85, Hercules (on the left) shows the reaction to a double-leg take-down attempt by Antaeus. He removes his legs from the range of the attack while "sprawling" his body on top of Antaeus' own. At the same time he tries to pass his arm in front of his opponent's neck to execute a reverse strangulation. However Antaeus reacts shrewdly, closing the gap, lifting his left arm next to his ear, at the same time pressing down with his left foot, preparing to rise.

The sequel to Hercules' attempt is shown in figure 3.86. The athlete on the right has completed the process of forcing his opponent to the ground, who has retreated into the position known today as "the turtle" in order to protect himself. From there on, regaining his base, he will counterattack with a double-leg takedown, by applying pressure with his head to the side, preparing to throw his opponent.

Figure 3.86. From the tombs at Beni Hasan, Egypt, 2000 BCE. (Drawing by P. E. Newberry, from the publication *Beni Hasan*, London, 1893.)

## CONTEMPORARY APPLICATIONS

### Penetrating for a Double-Leg Takedown

The attacker on the left infiltrates his opponent's defenses, entering between the legs of his opponent. During this breach of his opponent's defenses, he keeps his hands near his face as a guard in case of a possible counter blow (A–B).

He grabs his opponent right behind the knee joint without clasping his palms together (C).

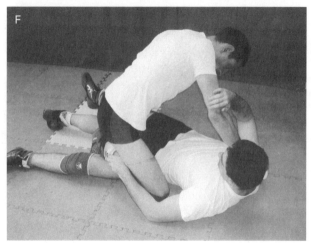

The throw is accomplished as he pulls with both hands and kneels down on his forward leg (D–E).

After the throw, he proceeds to establish a mounted position, taking care not to be caught between his opponent's legs (inside the opponent's "guard") (F–G).

## "Sprawl" (Counter to Attempt at Double-Leg Takedown)

The athlete on the left attacks by penetrating to grab both legs (A–B).

The opponent reacts by sliding his legs and body backward and placing the weight of his body on his opponent's back at the same time. He ends up on top of him, having pushed him down on his chest (C–D).

# ATTACKS TO THE NECK: CHOKES AND STRANGULATIONS

Figure 3.87a. Mosaic showing ancient wrestling ring. Roman era, Tusculum, Italy. (Drawing from *Monumenti ineditti pubblicati dall'Instituto di corrispondenze archeologica, 1857–63.*)

*"The Helians who supervise the games . . . praise the choke."*

PLATO'S SCHOLIAST

## ANALYSIS

Attacks using asphyxiating holds on the throat and neck, either chokes or strangulations, were considered superior technique in pankration, so whoever managed to apply such a difficult hold on a fellow competitor achieved acclaim. A choke is a technique in which pressure is applied directly to the trachea, obstructing the airway and causing suffocation. A strangulation is a technique which applies pressure to the areas around the trachea, squeezing the carotid arteries and windpipe and limiting blood flow to the brain. Both techniques are highly dangerous, can cause immediate unconsciousness and, when deliberately maintained, the death of the opponent.

Figure 3.87b, from the Roman mosaic above, depicts an excellent application of rear forearm choke. In this representation, the attacker has his back on the ground and has wrapped his legs in front of the defender, pinning him in place while he chokes him.

Figure 3.87b. Magnified part of the mosaic.

Figure 3.88a depicts a single-handed rear forearm choke attempt by the attacker on the left, while he holds the defender's left arm with his other hand. The defender is preparing to attack his opponent's groin using his free hand. Figure 3.88b shows the correct application of rear strangulation: the attacker has turned his body sideways and lifts the defender, who is unable to react and will lapse into unconsciousness.

a

b

Figure 3.88a, b. From tomb 17 at Beni Hasan, Egypt, 2000 BCE. (Drawings by P. E. Newberry, from the publication *Beni Hasan*, London, 1893.)

## Contemporary Applications

### Rear Strangulation

The attacker has passed his arm in front of the defender's neck, but is applying pressure to the sides of the neck, on one side with his forearm and on the other side with his bicep. The effectiveness of the hold is supported by tightening the arms in a grip that resembles a modern number 4 or triangle. This maneuver has become known as the "sleeper" hold today. The applied pressure is formidable and can block the carotid arteries (A).

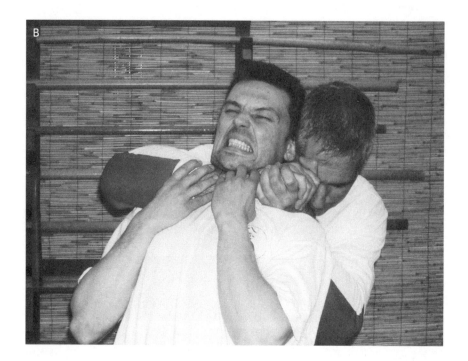

### Rear Forearm Choke

Pressure is applied by the forearm directly to the front of the throat, effectively blocking the trachea, or windpipe, of the defender (B). This is an extremely painful technique that also attacks the hyoid bone in the process and is very dangerous. In fact, it appears that the rear forearm choke was precisely the technique that brought about one of the few recorded deaths in ancient pankration, that of the athlete Arrichion, who refused to submit to his opponent's choke and broke his aggressor's ankle to escape, expiring in the process. (He was awarded victory posthumously.)

ANALYSIS OF THE TECHNIQUES
OF PANKRATION

# REVERSE FOREARM
# OR "GUILLOTINE" CHOKE

Figure 3.89. Roman bas-relief,
The Vatican Museum.

## ANALYSIS

Figure 3.89 is an excellent representation of a reverse choke. The centaur has trapped the attacker's head and—passing his forearm in front of his neck—he closes the hold, executing suffocation. The same technique is shown in figure 3.90, from Beni Hasan. In this case, the attacker was trapped while attempting a front leg takedown, and is being choked or strangled from a standing position.

Figure 3.90. From the tombs at Beni Hasan, Egypt, 2000 BCE. (Drawing by P. E. Newberry, from the publication *Beni Hasan*, London, 1893.)

ANALYSIS OF THE TECHNIQUES
OF PANKRATION

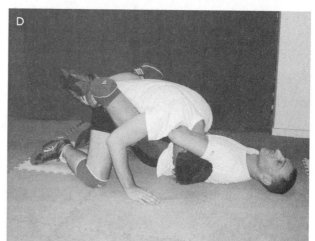

## CONTEMPORARY APPLICATIONS

### Reverse Forearm Choke (Guillotine) with a Fall

Many times—in submission wrestling competitions, for example—reverse chokes are finally fully secured while on the ground. This happens mainly after an attempt to grab the defender's legs, when the attacker manages to break the defender's balance and drive him to the ground (A–C).

However, a gap between his attacker's neck and his own body allows the defender (on the right) to pass his arm under his attacker's neck . . . and finish him off by trapping him between his legs, in a position called "the guard" in modern mixed martial arts (D). When executed in this fashion, reverse chokes actually attack the vertebrae, and can lead to hernia, dislocation, or more serious injuries; therefore, extreme care should be taken while applying these techniques.

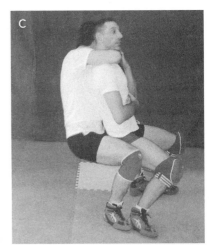

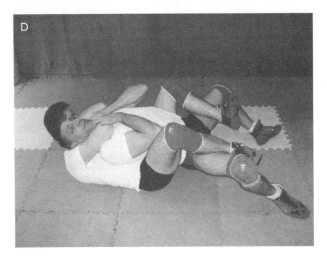

### "Naked" Rear Strangulation with a Takedown

The athlete on the left has applied a rear body clinch on his opponent (A).

From this position, he passes one arm around his opponent's neck and blocks his opponent's capability to step back with his own legs and feet (B).

Next, he breaks his opponent's balance and falls backward, taking his opponent with him by placing heel hooks inside his thighs. He finishes with a rear naked strangulation (C–D). This technique is commonly used in today's mixed martial arts.

# Ground Wrestling and Fighting

So far, we have analyzed standing combat and wrestling based on the archaeological archives. An important part of standing combat is its transfer to the ground. We have analyzed many techniques for throwing, lifting, sweeping, and taking down our opponent. We have also analyzed finishing holds in both the standing position and on the ground (when the entrapment range and the ground wrestling range coincide).

In this part we shall focus our attention on ground wrestling and fighting, where the fight usually ends in submission contests. Ground fighting is clearly part of an athletic contest (pankration)—like the submission fighting popular in mixed martial arts circles today—not part of the preparation for actual battle (pammachon).

We have already mentioned in a previous chapter that on an actual battlefield warriors had to avoid transferring the fight to the ground, due to the danger of being hurt by other members of the opposing army. Therefore, they focused on neutralizing their opponents by throwing them, by inflicting blows upon sensitive parts of their bodies, or by executing finishing holds in a standing position.

The other distinction between actual combat and athletic competitions is that in real combat the combatants carry weapons. In the ground fighting that occurs as a part of an athletic contest, there are certain positions that offer the advantage to those who achieve them, allowing them to follow up with finishing holds to win the contest. In conditions of real hand-to-hand combat in battle, which would presuppose the presence of short-range personal weapons, such positions could be fatal.

This is the basic difference between real battle arts and athletic duels. After all, the meaning of a duel is the confrontation between two persons (not two opposing armies). The kinesiology may seem similar but there are differences. The greatest difference is in the strategy, tactics, and application of fighting techniques in an athletic contest versus a real battle. In athletic competitions dangerous holds and other dangerous techniques, such as blows against sensitive body parts, are disallowed. Such techniques would be desirable in actual battle where the objective is to mortally wound the enemy. In athletic contests the safety of the athletes comes before everything else.

# THE MOUNTED POSITION

Figure 3.91a. Mosaic showing ancient wrestling ring. Roman era, Tusculum, Italy. (Drawing from *Monumenti ineditti pubblicati dall'Instituto di corrispondenze archeologica*, 1857–63.)

## ANALYSIS

The mounted position is a strong position in submission fighting, as it affords the attacker good control and mobility and allows hard blows with good placement. This position also restricts the upper body mobility of the defendant.

In submission wrestling, however, it is not as valuable, because it is not as stable as people would like to think. In judo, it is called *tate shiho gatame*.

### Armbar from the Mounted Position

In the Roman mosaic, the attacker keeps his opponent between his legs, but he does not sit on him; he remains standing. He seems to have trapped his opponent's arm. He has also armed his right hand and prepares to strike his opponent.

There are various options for attacking or applying finishing holds from a mounted position. Such attacks can take place against the opponent's neck and throat using asphyxiating holds. The defender's upper limbs are also vulnerable to dislocations of the elbow or shoulder.

Figure 3.91b. Magnification of a part of the mosaic.

Figure 3.92. From the tombs at Beni Hasan, Egypt, 2000 BCE. (Drawing by P. E. Newberry, from the publication *Beni Hasan*, London, 1893.)

## CONTEMPORARY APPLICATIONS

### Stabilization

Today, because the mounted position has become the premier ground-fighting position in mixed martial arts contests, it has changed significantly since ancient times. The mounted athlete strives to maintain his position by placing hooks under his opponents' legs (A). Sometimes he even places double hooks around his opponent's calves, restricting his own mobility (B). He presses his opponent toward the ground with his chest and, by spreading his hands far apart and placing them well in front of his body, he maintains a wide and steady base (A–B).

### Blows from a Mounted Position

The mounted position is desirable in a submission fight as it allows the attacker to hit his opponent effectively. From this position, having immobilized his opponent on the ground, the attacker finds himself in a favorable position for delivering direct downward blows (A–B).

### Direct Armbar with a Hook on the Neck

In submission fighting, when the defender tries to use his arms to block an attacker's blows from the riding position, the attacker is offered a good opportunity to trap and dislocate his opponent's elbow. He can place a hook on his opponent's neck with his leg and can finish the contest by holding the defender's arm with both hands (C). From this position, depending on his opponent's reaction, the attacker can cause a direct dislocation of the defender's elbow by falling sideways to the ground.

## Escape from the Mounted Position

The athlete under his opponent's mounted position tries to turn his attacker by trapping his arm on the side toward which he wants him to turn. The entrapment takes place by pulling the attacker's hand toward his ear (A–B).

Next he makes a bridge by pressing his feet into the ground near his hips and arching his back (C).

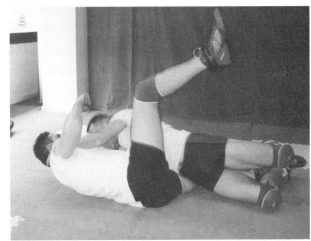

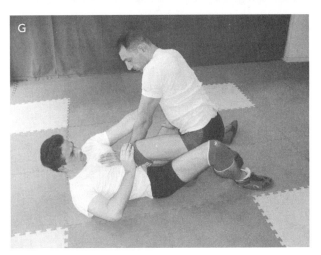

Then the defender turns his opponent toward his trapped arm and throws him to the floor (D–E).

As he finishes the throw, he is careful to control his opponent's free leg so as not to be trapped by it. (F).

Then he achieves a secure position with his knee between his opponent's legs, controlling him (G).

# REAR MOUNTED POSITION

### ANALYSIS

Figure 3.93. From the tombs at Beni Hasan, Egypt, 2000 BCE. (Drawing by P. E. Newberry, from the publication *Beni Hasan*, London, 1893.)

Figure 3.93 shows an exceptionally favorable position for the attacker. It is a position from which rear strangulation of his opponent can be accomplished. Also, besides favoring the most important hold for neutralizing his opponent, this position gives the attacker the option, as far as submission wrestling is concerned, to inflict blows against vital parts of his opponent's body. In ancient Greek pankration, blows from a rear mounted position prevailed as long as they were allowed by the regulations.

Escaping from this position is an exceptionally difficult task, especially when the attacker has placed hooks between his opponent's legs. This position offers the attacker a considerable advantage in combat, as well as in submission wrestling.

Figure 3.94. Greek statue, third century BCE, Galleria Uffizzi, Florence. (Drawing based on photograph from the museum.)

# REAR FOREARM CHOKE

## ANALYSIS

This is an important representation of superior technique in a pankration contest. The athlete beneath his opponent has retreated to the "turtle" position to protect himself from blows, chokes, and joint locks. However his opponent has managed to place hooks on both his legs, making it very hard for him to escape. Furthermore, the attacker has passed his left arm below the defender's neck; it is almost certain he will be forced to resign, at the risk of potential strangulation.

## CONTEMPORARY APPLICATION

### Rear "Naked" Forearm Choke and Strangulation

The attacker on top is attempting to "open" up his opponent with blows in order to pass his forearm under this throat and attempt a rear naked choke or strangulation (A).

He manages to pass his forearm under his opponent's windpipe and attempts a choke (B).

Figure 3.95. Pankration. Roman oil lamp, first century CE, Museo Nationale delle Terme, Rome. (Drawing based on photograph from the museum.)

Unable to secure an effective position, he modifies the choke to a strangulation, employing the "Figure 4" strangulation outlined earlier (C).

As the defender attempts to rise, the attacker passes heel "hooks" under
his thighs. From this position, it is extremely difficult to escape. Even if the
defender manages to turn, he will still be within his opponent's hold and
unable to counter (D).

# "GUARD" POSITION AND TRANSITION

Left. Figure 3.96. From tomb 15 at Beni Hasan, Egypt, 2000 BCE. (Drawing by P. E. Newberry, from the publication *Beni Hasan*, London, 1893.)

Right. Figure 3.97. From tomb 15 at Beni Hasan, east wall (plate 5), Egypt, 2000 BCE. (Drawing by P. E. Newberry, from the publication *Beni Hasan*, London, 1893.)

## ANALYSIS

The "guard" position (using contemporary mixed martial arts terminology) shown in figure 3.96 is the desired position when an athlete has his back to the ground. It allows him to control the mobility of his opponent, to launch final attacks, to defend against blows and holds, and to reverse the position and get on top of him. A distinction is made between an open or closed position, depending on whether he has entangled his legs around his opponent. The "guard" offers adequate stability, plus the possibility to transpose to a more favorable position, such as the mounted position or the side hold-down position. But the opponent has a similar chance if he can "pass the guard," to use modern terminology.

Figure 3.97 shows the transition from a guard position (passing the guard) to a side hold-down position. The athlete on the left has broken his opponent's guard, and, holding one of his legs from below, is preparing to transition to a side hold-down position, known in judo as *yoko shiho gatame*.

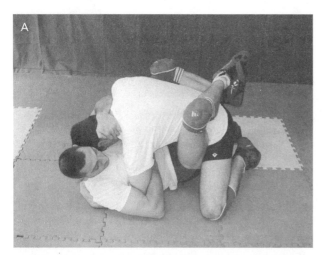

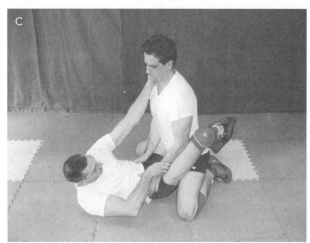

## Contemporary Application

### Passing the Guard Position and Transition to Side Hold-Down* Position

The athlete on top is caught in his opponent's guard position (A).

He attempts to crawl backward, while holding on to his opponent's arms, pressing his biceps (B).

Keeping his head and body at a safe distance, he firmly presses his opponent's pelvis down to the ground (C).

---

*In this book, we have deliberately used the term *hold down* rather than *pin,* due to the connotations in modern wrestling in which a pin equals victory. There is no such case of victory due to a pin in submission wrestling; rather, it is a stable position from which further maneuvers to insure victory can be initiated.

Next, he places one knee under his opponent's pelvis, while he steps back with the other leg (D).

He proceeds to control his opponent's leg on his own shoulder and with his right arm holds his opponent's opposite shoulder. He uses his left arm to keep his opponent's other leg on the ground (E).

By shaking the defender's leg off his shoulder he transfers to and finishes with the side hold-down position (F).

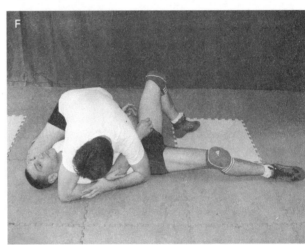

Figure 3.98. From tomb 15 at Beni Hasan, east wall, Egypt, 2000 BCE. (Drawing by P. E. Newberry, from the publication *Beni Hasan*, London, 1893.)

# TRIANGULAR STRANGULATION

## ANALYSIS

Nowadays, triangular strangulation, shown in figure 3.98, is considered among the most powerful and difficult techniques for eliminating an opponent. Triangular strangulation with the legs is a technique that is applied usually after a defendant's guard position has been broken, when the attacker has not trapped both of the defendant's legs after breaking the guard. With a degree of sadness and awe, we came to discover that the standard of technique in 2000 BCE was much superior than it is today.

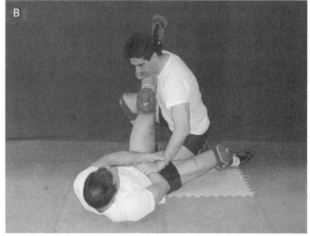

## CONTEMPORARY APPLICATION

The triangular strangulation is usually executed after the defender's guard position is broken. As the attacker attempts to go into a side hold-down position, as shown previously, the defender pulls his opponent's arm (A–B).

He locks his legs tightly with a "Figure 4" hold. This way he accomplishes strangulation with his opponent's arm and the entanglement of his legs (C).

# HALF-GUARD POSITION

## ANALYSIS

Many of the images drawn on the walls of the tombs at Beni Hasan depict ground wrestling. It would have been strange if the half-guard position were missing. This position is almost as valuable as the full guard position. However, it allows the athlete on top added chances to transfer to a more favorable position.*

## CONTEMPORARY APPLICATION

In the half-guard position it is important to control the opponent's balance at all times in order to topple him over or escape from him at an opportune moment (A).

The athlete on the bottom applies a Figure 4 leg position, which allows for quick bridges† and transitions (B).

Figures 3.99, 3.100. From tomb 15 at Beni Hasan, east wall (plate 5), Egypt, 2000 BCE. (Drawings by P. E. Newberry, from the publication *Beni Hasan*, London, 1893.)

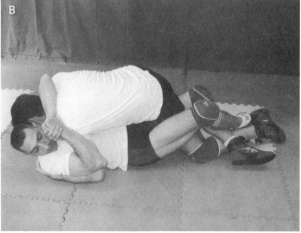

---

*This might not be the case in actual combat, where the half-guard is often a more suitable position for controlling an opponent who has taken us to the ground, without exposing our genitals. That having been said, the half-guard requires a higher degree of skill to use.

†A "bridge" in wrestling is a maneuver during which we arch our back while on the ground in order to "throw" the opponent over us.

# FOUR-POINTS POSITION

Figure 3.101. From tomb 17 at Beni Hasan, east wall (plate 15), Egypt, 2000 BCE. (Drawing by P. E. Newberry, from the publication *Beni Hasan*, London, 1893.)

## ANALYSIS

The "four-points" position is a very solid position for submission wrestling on the ground but with limited attacking options. This position is known in contemporary judo practice as *kami shiho gatame*.*

## CONTEMPORARY APPLICATION

A good opportunity to go to the four-points position occurs after sprawling the opponent on the ground following a takedown attempt to grab our legs. With the opponent in a "turtle" position, the athlete on the left turns him over and follows up by consolidating his position.

---

*In contemporary wrestling or judo, this position would be considered a pin and lead to victory, but in submission wrestling its value is merely that of a stable position.

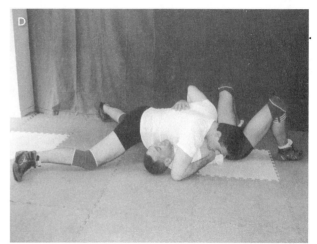

First the attacker passes one arm under his opponent's arms (A).

Then the attacker pushes downward with his leg, placing his foot near his opponent's head (B).

Clasping his palms behind his opponent's back, he turns him over (C).

He finishes with a four-points hold-down position (D).

# HEADLOCK POSITION

Figure 3.102. From tomb 17 at Beni Hasan, east wall, Egypt, 2000 BCE. (Drawing by P. E. Newberry, from the publication *Beni Hasan*, London, 1893.)

## ANALYSIS

Although we have referred to this position in the section on standing submission wrestling, we shall expand a little as it is actually a better position for ground fighting. It is known in judo as the *kesa gatame* position. In pure submission wrestling (where no strikes to the opponent are allowed), it is not considered a worthwhile position, as the defender can rather easily escape and proceed to a dangerous counterattack. However, in pankration (submission fighting) it is a more powerful position, as the attacker is in a situation where he can readily deliver blows to the opponent, having gravity on his side.*

## CONTEMPORARY APPLICATION

Blows from a headlock position (A).

---

*It is also a very useful position in close-quarter combat.

# KNEE ON THE ABDOMEN POSITION

Figures 3.103, 3.104. From tombs 17–15 at Beni Hasan, east wall, Egypt, 2000 BCE. (Drawings by P. E. Newberry, from the publication *Beni Hasan*, London, 1893.)

## ANALYSIS

This position's main trait is mediocre stability, coupled with multiple options for attack and exceptional mobility. The attacker can execute both blows and holds from this position, which is quite useful and popular in today's no-holds-barred contests. Blows are dealt in order to loosen up the defender's guard and to open the way for the attacker to trap a limb and proceed to a finishing hold. The supporting leg may be slightly bent or kept straight.

## CONTEMPORARY APPLICATION

Repeated blows are dealt to the opponent from the "Knee on the Abdomen" position (A).

# KNEE AND CALF
# DISLOCATIONS (LEGLOCKS)

Dislocating and/or finishing* leg locks are not really prevalent in the martial arts of the East and the combat sports that have been generated from them. But in a martial art or a combat sport where few restrictive rules apply, such as submission wrestling and pankration (submission fighting), leg locks are powerful tools in the athlete's or fighter's arsenal. Therefore, in the Beni Hasan frescoes as well as in the rest of the archaeological archives (Greco-Roman), there are representations that denote not just the existence of such techniques but also very advanced technical knowledge of the subject. They take different forms, such as dislocating knee holds (direct and complex dislocations), dislocating ankle holds (utilizing twisting movements), and pain-inflicting holds that force the defender to resign.

It is worth mentioning that compared to the upper limbs, legs have fewer nerves, taking their mass into consideration. For this reason, pain appears abruptly in leg locks. If the defending athlete does not have the correct technical knowledge that allows him to know when to resign the contest before it is too late, serious injury might be the outcome.†

---

*A finishing move causes termination of the contest or injury as the opponent chooses.
†For this reason, leg locks are forbidden in many combat sports such as contemporary wrestling and modern judo. They are utilized extensively in Russian *sambo*.

# DIRECT KNEE
# DISLOCATION WITH A FALL

Figures 3.105, 3.106. From tomb 15 (plate 16), east wall, at Beni Hasan, Egypt, 2000 BCE. (Drawings by P. E. Newberry, from the publication *Beni Hasan*, London, 1893.)

## ANALYSIS

These two representations from Beni Hasan are really impressive! They confirm that nothing has changed over the millennia. The demonstration of this technique would be exactly the same today. In figure 3.105, the attacker holding his opponent's leg seems to be trying to force him to the ground to immobilize him and oblige him to resign. In figure 3.106 it is obvious that the attacker, having bent his torso forward and stretched his legs, intends to finish off his opponent standing up. The dislocation is executed by overextending the opponent's leg, which causes serious damage to his joint, mainly the rupture of the ligaments.

## Contemporary Application

One athlete is in a position of rear body hold. The defender reacts at first with a "jackknife"* and then he moves a little sideways, in order to bring his opponent's leg between his legs (A–B).

Next, he bends down and holds his opponent's leg with both hands (C).

---

*In submission wrestling the "jackknife" is a defensive move that an athlete makes when his opponent has executed a rear body hold on him. He lowers his pelvis a little lower than his opponent's pelvis by opening his legs. This move prevents his opponent from lifting him off the ground.

 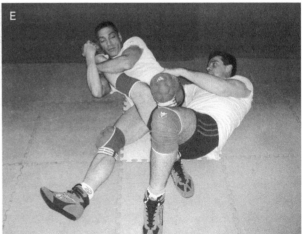

As he lifts it upward, he forces his opponent to fall and he follows him to the ground (D).

He sits on his opponent's pelvis, and, holding his opponent's leg stretched against his chest, he falls sideways and pulls (E).

# DIRECT KNEE DISLOCATION ON THE GROUND

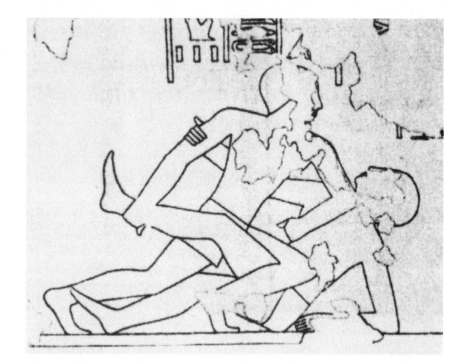

Figure 3.107. Senbi tomb, Meir, Egypt, 2000 BCE. (From the book *The Rock Tombs of Meir*, by Aylward M. Blackman, London: Egypt Exploration Society, 1914.)

## ANALYSIS

Here are three excellent representations of leg attacks, all from Egypt. In order to execute a direct knee dislocation, the attacker must "nail down" his opponent's pelvis to the ground. This is what the athlete on the left seems to be doing in figure 3.107. At the same time, he hits his opponent's chin with his elbow. In figures 3.108 and 3.109, the dark figure seems to be in a preparatory stage for executing a direct knee dislocation.

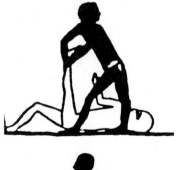

Figures 3.108, 3.109. From tomb 15, east wall, at Beni Hasan, Egypt, 2000 BCE. (Drawings by P. E. Newberry, from the publication *Beni Hasan*, London, 1893.)

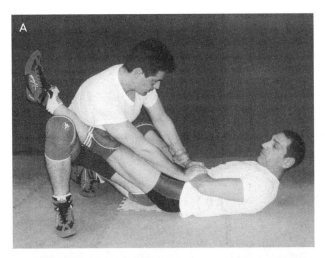

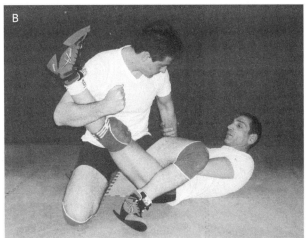

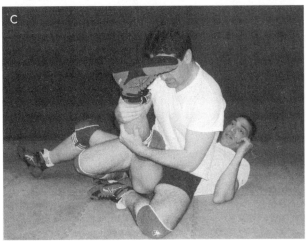

## Contemporary Application

First the athlete on the left breaks the defender's guard position (A).

Then, the attacker immediately bends his knee over his opponent's trapped leg (B).

Next, he holds the leg with both hands (C).

Falling on his side, he pulls hard, keeping his opponent's leg trapped between his legs (D).

# TIBIO-FIBULAR ATTACKS

Figure 3.110. From tomb 29, south wall (plate 23), at Beni Hasan, Egypt, 2000 BCE. (Drawing by P. E. Newberry, from the publication *Beni Hasan*, London, 1893.)

## ANALYSIS

In ground wrestling and ground fighting, there are certain positions that are much preferred by athletes. Most of the time, these positions cannot be clearly distinguished by someone who is not familiar with the contest's intricacies, and are considered random positions in the course of the contest. However, nothing happens at random in submission contests, and the ancient Egyptians were fully aware of this; the unknown artist of Beni Hasan has offered us yet again one more revealing image. In figure 3.110 the attacker, after having thrown his opponent to the ground, has obviously executed a reverse rear mounted position and is preparing to apply a hold on his opponent's calf (tibio-fibular region). We cannot be certain whether he is preparing to apply pressure to the soft tissues of the calf, or twist the lower leg itself to attack the related joints.

## CONTEMPORARY APPLICATION

After an attempted kick, the defender arrests his opponent's leg and proceeds to counterattack, throwing his opponent (A–B).

He continues to hold his leg and takes precautions not to be caught in a half guard position, keeping his opponent's other leg against the ground, with his opposite hand (C).

After securing his opponent's leg by trapping it under his armpit, he continues with an inward turn, passing his leg over the defender (D).

He finishes by sitting on his opponent, in a reverse rear mounted position, tightening his hold around his opponent's leg and applying pressure to the soft tissues (E).

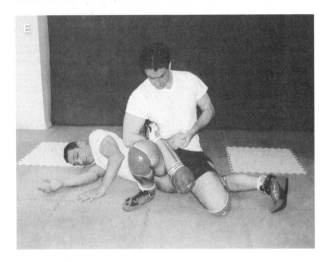

ANALYSIS OF THE TECHNIQUES
OF PANKRATION

# TWISTING ANKLE/KNEE DISLOCATION (HEEL HOOK)

## ANALYSIS

Figure 3.111. Roman bas-relief, the Vatican Museum.

This excellent representation from the Roman archive depicts an ankle dislocation hold, using a twisting move. This hold is essentially a counter move, as it is very difficult for the attacker to catch his opponent's leg in this fashion. It therefore seems that the centaur managed to catch the leg and throw his opponent while the latter attempted a kick. The injury that is inflicted, provided there are no gaps in the hold, would affect the knee joint first, as the knee will turn along with the twisting movement applied to the tibio-fibular region of the lower leg. As the knee joint is not as flexible as the ankle joint, it will be damaged first, followed by the ankle.

## CONTEMPORARY APPLICATION

In this demonstration the technique is performed on the ground as a counter move, after an attempted leg attack by the opponent and, specifically, pressure on the soft part of the calf. This is a defensive counter, which is applied in similar conditions in submission contests today. An athlete may tolerate the pain in the calf muscle caused by his opponent's attack for a while, but the same does not hold true for the twisting/dislocating hold he applies to the other athlete's ankle joint. As we mentioned earlier, pain and injury will probably be felt first at the knee joint, and, due to the anatomical limitations of the nervous system in the leg, by the time the pain is felt, injury may well have occurred; this is a problem with such techniques in athletic competitions.

The athlete on the right has trapped his opponent's leg and applies pressure to the soft part of the calf. However his own leg is exposed in the wrong position (a frequent error especially among athletes whose knowledge is somewhat incomplete) (A).

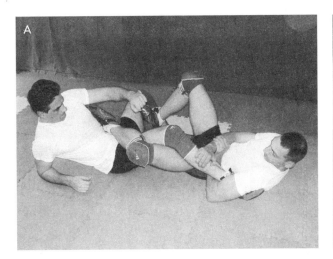

The athlete on the left reacts by rising slightly to relieve his leg from the pain and pushing down with his other hand captures his opponent's heel and traps it under his armpit (B).

Next, he falls back again holding tightly and twisting his opponent's ankle and knee joints (C).

# 4 ⬥➤ THE INNER PATH

All of the mental effort that produced this book would be fruitless had we not examined the evolution and the psyche of the warriors who developed pammachon during the Bronze Age, in order to focus on the existence (or not) of an inner spiritual path pursued by these fighters. The possibility of doing this might at first seem inconceivable—how could we examine the psyche of people who do not exist anymore and have not left behind any kind of concrete evidence of their inner world?

The answer to this question lies in the same process that enabled us to recreate ancient combat techniques, that is, a close examination of the archaeological archives and recognition of the fact that the functions of the human body are the same after ten thousand years. Similarly, we believe that we can reproduce the inner world of our ancestors with the same approach by exploring existing esoteric practices in the context of archaeological evidence of ancient spiritual rituals and mythological references. Looking at the facts under this spectrum reveals that the inner path of the ancient fighters is evident and real, and that it originated in the Neolithic Age, with the expansion of shamanism and the transfer of spiritual rituals from the worship of female deities of the earth and fertility to the worship of male gods of the heavens and thunder. The aim of this inquiry is also clear: technology has led modern life to a dead end. It may be beneficial to individuals and to society as a whole to study the activities of "primitive" peoples in order to rediscover a source of vitality and psychological health.

# SHAMANISM'S SPIRALS AND CAVES

In order to examine this spiritual path in depth, we must take into account the progress of contemporary biophysics and recent experiments and research. We shall be able to fully comprehend the wisdom of our ancient ancestors with the aid of recent scientific discoveries and contemporary theories on physics and consciousness alone. However, as a first step, we shall tread on the path of religion.

Shamanism was the first religion of sentient human beings, a religion whose concepts still persist among contemporary religions. Although the word *shaman* comes from the tribe of the Tungus nomads from Siberia, there is no doubt that the roots of this religion are European or North African, and that, generally speaking, it originated throughout the larger area of the Mediterranean basin.* It seems that shamanism appeared in the first years of the Paleolithic in Europe, between 30,000 and 15,000 BCE, and spread to Asia and America (through Alaska) between 11,000 and 8000 BCE.

The central idea of shamanism is that the universe consists of two connected worlds: the material world and the spiritual world. Those who live in the material world are influenced by the spiritual world. The forces of the spiritual world can be either ancestors or non-human entities, gods, or demons, who bring people good or bad luck, health or death. Therefore, a middleman is needed, who, like a good diplomat, communicates with the entities of the spiritual world and appeases them on behalf of the humans. This middleman is none other than the shaman. Through the shaman humans received guidance and advice from the spiritual world to improve their standard of living.

Shamanism's belief in two parallel, connected worlds probably influenced the course of more recent religious beliefs worldwide. Two vital motifs are met with regularly in the archaeological documents on shamanism, and both are directly connected with this study. The first one is the worldwide presence of spiral depictions, in places where there is shamanic influence in local religions. The second is the shamanistic worship of caves and underground spaces.

Let us start with the second motif. The idea of a connection between the spiritual world and the inside of the earth is as old as humankind. The

---

*Joseph Campbell, *The Way of the Animal Powers: Mythologies of the Great Hunt* (New York: Harper and Row, 1988).

fact that Paleolithic and Neolithic humans considered caves as places of worship may have arisen from their observation of the ease with which shamans contacted the spiritual world while inside the earth. Anthropologists have discovered the most ancient cathedral in the world in the depths of the Tuc D'Audoubert cave in France, almost a mile below the earth's surface. The findings date back to 13,000 BCE. Why did the pilgrims have to undergo the ordeal of crawling for a mile below the earth's surface, through narrow passages? In Greece, the famous oracle at Acheron—where pilgrims went to speak with the spirits of their dead ancestors—is nothing more than a deeply dug hole in the ground.

On the island of Crete, at Chania Cape on the Akroteri peninsula, there is another cave that illustrates the timelessness of this phenomenon. There are two Christian Orthodox monasteries in the vicinity of this cave. On the coast is Katholikos Monastery, built in the sixth century CE, which was deserted several centuries later due to pirate attacks. Higher up on the mountain, the monks built Gouverneto Monastery in the twelfth century CE. Roughly 300 yards down the road from the Gouverneto Monastery, between the locations of the old and the newer monasteries, there is a huge cave, at the entrance of which a small church has been built. A remarkable feature of this cave is a very large stalagmite in the central hall, which has the unmistakable shape of a bear. Archaeological research has proven that humans have made use of the cave of the Gouverneto monastery for at least 10,000 years. Neolithic people worshipped the Bear of the Caves and Mother Earth there.

In the age of the Minoan civilization the cave was dedicated to Dictynna, a Cretan virgin goddess whose totem was the bear. In the classical era Dictynna was replaced by Artemis (the Roman Diana), one more virgin goddess for whom the bear was sacred. (We shall see later that the form of Artemis as Potnia Theron, or "Mistress of the Animals," is directly related to the shamanistic motif.) When the Greeks of that area adopted Christianity (fourth to sixth centuries) the cave was dedicated to Panagia Arkoudiotissa (the Virgin Mary of the Bears) and a water tank was built on the stalagmite for christenings, supplied by a little spring at the base. It is obvious that the goddess that was worshipped in the cave over the past 4,000 years had her name changed several times, but not her essence, something that has happened to many cultural features of Greece.

Of course the phenomenon of "sacred caves" is not exclusively a Greek feature; it is characteristic of all peoples in all geographical areas of the world. There is evidence of the correlation between underground spaces and contact with the spiritual world in China, India, North and South America, the Middle East and, naturally, central Europe, dating from the early archaic age onward.

Besides the caves, there is another motif evident worldwide as a result of the expansion of shamanism: the helix and the spiral helix. Morphologically this motif often takes the shape of a swastika, or its counterpart, the yin-yang symbol made popular by Chinese culture. The swastika and the spiral helix present a symbol that can be found all over the world in archaeological findings from very ancient times; they are seen in Indian, Greek, Chinese, North and South American, Mesopotamian, Persian, and European excavations. What is indeed a wonder is how ancient peoples could understand that the spiral helix is a form that governs life in general and the space-time of our galaxy: our DNA, the structural element of our bodies, bears the structure of a double spiral helix, and our galaxy has the shape of a spiral helix with a central "compressed" spherical mass with four arms, more or less resembling a swastika!

The frequent depiction of the helix by so many ancient peoples probably means that they also knew that the helix is a basic element of our existence in the material world (and perhaps beyond). In Greek, the word *exelixi* ("evolution") comes from *ex helikos* ("from the helix"), which is most impressive in itself.* The spiral helix is very significant in our organism as a whole, not only in our DNA. The "conveyors" inside our cells consist of spiral helixes of the protein tubulin, which are called microtubules. Microtubules were discovered in a study of single cell organisms, which do not have nervous systems, in the effort to determine how they make decisions and receive information, in other words, how these living organisms think. There is a theory that in multicellular organisms microtubules form a local nervous system in each individual cell, so that it can have its own autonomous communication with every other cell of the body.

Microtubules certainly play their part in the cohesion and communication system throughout our organism. The existence of microtubules may also explain another phenomenon that has been observed experimentally in the past twenty years: the cells of an organism

---

*Even more intriguing in the context of the martial arts is the connection between the word *elikas* (helix) with its contemporary meaning of *elissomai* (maneuver), that is, "I move spirally, I avoid, I absorb, I divert."

have memory. Recipients of transplanted organs, especially hearts, frequently acquire the wishes, preferences, and fears of the donor. It seems that—besides our nervous system—*we also think with our body,* which is something Far Eastern populations in particular have known for thousands of years. It is quite possible that microtubules and the spiral helix may provide the solution to the paradox of this experimentally observed phenomenon.

The form of the spiral helix that originates in the shape of our galaxy and culminates in our own DNA, with many levels in between, may explain fractally many properties of space-time, matter, and possibly our own consciousness. It is not by chance that indigenous populations came to the same conclusion tens of thousands of years ago. Lacking in the technological knowledge of today, they turned inward, using consciousness as a sense organ, because, according to modern physics, consciousness plays a major part in the shaping of space-time.*

## GRAVITY VS. NUCLEAR FUSION

In January 2003, it was experimentally proven that the speed of gravity is equal to the speed of light, confirming Einstein's equations. This evidence is substantial for the model we present in this chapter. Basically, this experiment proved that the expansive force of the electromagnetic spectrum (including light), generated by the stars, equalizes the forces of gravity and dark matter in the universe, giving shape to space-time.

Contemporary science accepts the principle that, if there were no nuclear fusion to counterbalance gravity with its expansive force, our sun would have collapsed long ago, under the weight of its own gravity. This means that all stars are battlefields, where gravity fights against an unknown force that causes nuclear fusion, and that this battle between two polar opposites determines the form of our own space-time.†

---

*John Archibald Wheeler, with Kenneth Ford, *Geons, Black Holes and Quantum Foam: A Life in Physics* (New York: W. W. Norton & Company, 1998).

†Astrophysicist Robert Kirshner, Clowes Professor of Science at Harvard University, believes that the existence of dark matter, spread around the universe, can explain the observed distortions of space-time and the acceleration of the galaxies in the universe. He speaks of a "so far unknown form of dark matter" and of an "acceleration of the galaxies due to a repulsion by masses of dark matter"—one more manifestation of the bipolar nature of the universe.

"War is the father of all," Heracleitos wrote. When considering gravity, most of us remember the basics we learned in high school: that a mass exercises pulling power on another mass and this is the reason we fall to the ground when we lose our balance. But let us further analyze this principle, to offer a clearer description of this phenomenon: gravity is a force that wants to make all the matter in the universe collapse and be condensed to a single mass (and then into one singularity).*

The nuclear fusion inherent to the stars is the expansive force that opposes gravity and keeps space-time in existence (in stars, nuclear fusion "wins" the battle against gravity, resulting in the generation and outflow of energy in the electromagnetic spectrum).

*War is the father of all.* Our world is fractal in its nature. It is logical to accept as true that whatever happens in the macrocosm, happens in the microcosm. Is it possible that a battle that forms the central tenet of the universe's substance would not reflect itself in our own existence as individuals?

All ancient populations believed that it did.

In ancient civilizations—probably influenced by the first global religion, shamanism—people believed the world was ruled by *two opposing forces (or "breaths")* in the universe. The Chinese call these opposing forces yin and yang. The ancient Greeks spoke of Father Uranus and Mother Earth, about the "endless" and "form"; the Navajo of North America made corresponding references. The Indians and

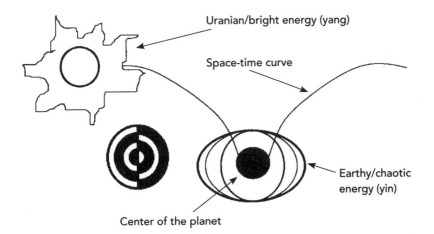

Figure 4.1. Two opposing forces

---

*A singularity is that entity in physics that represents a mass so large it is beyond the constructs of space-time. In popular terms, this is called a black hole.

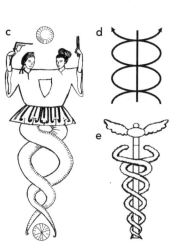

Figure 4.2. The spiral twisting together of the two universal forces on a stationary wave determines our existence, our karma: a) presentation on a vase at the Louvre, b) the *chakra* and *nadi* system of Hindu mysticism, c) reproduction from a wall drawing in a Chinese Taoist sanctum, d) the stationary wave in physics, and e) Hermes' caduceus.

Tibetans spoke of a lunar and solar breath. It is interesting that all of these ancient peoples focused on the idea that both forces—yin and yang—transmit their energy in the form of *breath* to the entire universe. The ancient Chinese spoke of *chi*, the ancient Greeks of *pneuma* (within the context of a material substance that "evaporates," like alcohol—in fact alcohol in Greek is called *oinopneuma*—"wine breath"), the Romans of *spiritus*, the Hebrews of *ruach*, the Tibetans of *rlung*, the Indians of *prana*. Strangely enough, all of the above-mentioned words mean "air," "steam," "breath," "a material substance that evaporates." According to the Eastern theory—which (based on the archaeological evidence regarding the sacred caves already mentioned) may have preserved some even older world wide creeds—yin ascends from the center of the earth, while yang falls upon us like a bright breath from our sun.

On the wall of a Chinese temple in Java is a thought-provoking depiction of yin and yang. Instead of the well-known circular black and white depiction of yin and yang, familiar to the Western world, here the artist depicts the two energies as lovers, two dragons in a close embrace (figure 4.2c). The caduceus, depicting two snakes wrapped around a stick, is an ancient symbol widely spread all over ancient Greece, which was related to heralds and the god Hermes (figure 4.2e). The most ancient depiction of a caduceus that survives is in the Louvre, on a Mesopotamian vase (figure 4.2a), which also depicts two dragons around a central axis and dates to the second millennium BCE. It is really amazing that this symbol has been adopted by Orthodox Christianity and has become, in its simple form, the Archbishop's and Patriarch's crosier (figure 4.3). What does this symbol depict? Two streams of energy, wrapped together like lovers?

No doubt, but something more important may be determined from such symbols. The key to this puzzle can be found in the presentations of wall drawings of Hindu Tantra, specifically those that are preserved from the Tantric Buddhism of Tibet starting from the eighth century CE. According to Eastern mysticism, human substance is determined by two powers that flow into channels *(nadis)* and wrap together in knots *(chakras)*. One type of energy is perceived as solar, coming from the sun, and the other one as chthonic or lunar (and we can see again that there is a universal correlation of Earth worship and the moon's phases), coming from the center of the earth. The entanglement of

Figure 4.3. It is highly likely that the Archbishop's crosier in Orthodox Christianity relates back to the same helical entwining of energies that is referenced by all ancient civilizations. The symbol was adopted by the church as a result of Neoplatonic influences on Christianity during its development into an organized religion. Painting from the Greek Orthodox Patriarchate of Alexandria in Egypt. (Photograph by Kostas Dervenis.)

these two energies determines the energetic make-up of each individual. These energies form seven main knots (chakras) on the central body axis. In and around each chakra each of these energies moves separately in a spiral helix direction, in its own individual channel (while on the main axis both energies can move together). It does not seem illogical to suggest that these symbols depict standing waves of the two universal energies, similar to the standing wave one can see on an oscilloscope in such cases.

## HARNESSING THE POWERS WITHIN

Considering the fractal expansion of the helix in our universe, and the fact that contemporary astrophysics has established that space-time is formed by the confrontation of two polar opposite powers, let us try to understand the beliefs of ancient populations. This task requires the use of more data and suggestions.

"Form (the Finite) and the Infinite coexist within ourselves," according to Plato.* We shall return to this phrase of the great wrestler, after we have examined the beliefs of the ancients on this subject. As we have seen, the emphasis on the spiral entanglement of the two energies was found worldwide. This may offer an explanation regarding the myths of demi-gods and heroes told by all ancient peoples around the world. We dare suggest this for the following reason: the violation of limitations inherent to our existing biophysical model, as well as what may be called "superhuman powers," has already been proven as attainable by human beings within a laboratory environment, their extraordinary powers the result of esoteric exercise and development.

An amazing discovery followed scientific studies done in the eighties. Professor Herbert Benson of the Harvard Medical School, visiting remote Himalayan monasteries, certified that there were Tibetan monks who could increase the temperature of their fingers and toes by 17 degrees Fahrenheit, that is, up to 115 degrees. It is noteworthy that, normally, a human being suffers irreversible neurological damage and his life is in danger when his body temperature exceeds 108 degrees. In 1985, researchers in Benson's team filmed half-naked monks overnight, who repeatedly dried three-by-six-foot wet sheets soaked in cold water (49 degrees Fahrenheit) using their increased body temperature, in a room where the temperature was 40 degrees Fahrenheit; in the process steam was produced from the heat (it took the monks about one hour to dry each sheet)! Next, they filmed monks outside the monastery, meditating half naked (wearing only one thin cotton garment, leaving

---

*Plato, *Philibos,* 16c.

one shoulder uncovered) on a Tibetan highland, at an altitude of 15,000 feet and a certified temperature of zero degrees Fahrenheit (not counting the freezing influence of the wind-chill factor on the highlands!). The monks were squatting on the frozen ground meditating, not in contact with each other, and there was no indication of shivering or trembling. There is no explanation for this phenomenon, according to the existing biophysical model.

Benson also discovered that these monks could lower their metabolism by up to 64 percent, which is unbelievable. This observation may prove significant as we proceed with our analysis.

These Tibetan monks of Tantric Buddhism are called *repa,* meaning "those who wear cotton," and in fact a white cotton robe is the very desirable reward for their training. The meditation exercise they use is called *gTummo* ("wild woman") and has three essential components: 1) holding and suppressing the breath in the center of the lower abdomen; 2) sexual temperance; and 3) transforming sexual energy through meditation into another form of energy, in this case thermal energy. The mental (and possibly physical?) model they use during concentration and meditation is exactly identical to that of the spiral entanglement of the two energies referred to above. They believe that they achieve these admirable and "supernatural" results by controlling the concentration, entanglement, and dispersion of the two breaths: "solar" (father energy) and "lunar" (mother energy) in their bodies.

We remind the reader that the main reason we refer to this model is that it offers a likely explanation for the "supernatural" powers recorded in the ancient myths. There is evidence, based on the archaeological record, that this indeed is so. In Sanskrit that energy which comes from the transformation of sexual energy is called *kundalini,* which means "coiled energy" and is symbolized by a snake coiled around the base of the spine (it is referred to as "the snake power"). The correlation of the snake in all ancient religious and mystical traditions to this type of "breath" energy most likely originates from a single source.

The method of these practices—known in Chinese as *neikung,* "esoteric force"—is the focusing and activation of the energy center that is placed at the center of the lower abdomen, called *dantien* in Chinese, *hara* in Japanese, *svadhisthana chakra* in Sanskrit, and so forth. Greek archeological archives may document similar practices. At the Herakleion Museum, in Crete, for example, there are the famous statuettes of the Minoan priestesses, wrapped up in snakes. The manner in which the snakes are wrapped around the arms of one priestess, and the "knot" at the point of the energy center of the lower abdomen, lead us to the conclusion that this depicts the same technique that is used by the *repa* monks. Further, the corset that the priestess is wearing below her breasts has the same shape as the caduceus, showing the spiral entanglement of the two energies! Can this be coincidental?

Further consideration of the literary and archaeological archives with reference to the practices mentioned reveals some important clues regarding the psychic methods of the warriors in the Bronze Age: they indicate that the universal practice of transforming sexual energy, probably deriving from shamanism thousands of years ago, built the foundations of the hero-worship that exists in all ancient cultures.

The connection between the sexual act and the ritual of the duel derives from Nature, occurring annually, during the mating time of the species. Archaeological archives confirm that the relation between battle and reproduction was bequeathed to the human species. For example, in the Gilf Kebir caves at the border between southwest Egypt and Libya, Neolithic drawings from 7000 BCE demonstrate an obvious connection between the ritual duel and sexual reproduction. In figure 4.5a, two men fight a bloody battle with axes and knives, while right below them other men participate in a wrestling athletic confrontation similar to the contemporary Japanese *sumo* wrestling (next to them there is a chorus of women, watching and judging the activities). In figure 4.5b two men, wearing phalli reminiscent of the Dionysian rites in ancient Greece, are entangled in an athletic duel that is clearly a boxing contest. Other images from archaeological archives confirm that there has been a continuous correlation between religious activities, ritual duels, and sexuality and fertility throughout the ages. This can still be seen today in the wrestling contests that accompany various religious festivities throughout the world.

The heroes of the Bronze Age, the warrior elite, were distinguished by being the only humans who had the psychic strength and will power to undertake and undergo the ordeal of transforming vital energy. Their rarity is simple—this practice requires control of sexual desire, either by abstention or through a non-orgasmic sexual act. The Mycenaean Greek myth about Hercules (Herakles in Greek) refers clearly to the drawing of

Figure 4.4. Statuette of a Minoan priestess, seventeenth century BCE, Herakleion Museum, Crete.

strength from the two universal energies when he was a baby, and thus pure of heart. As mentioned earlier, the name Hercules means "Hera's glory." Hera is a manifestation of the Mother Goddess whose name means "worthy" and has similar roots to the word "hero." In the relevant myth, it is mentioned that Hera persecuted Hercules, yet he carries her name. Isn't this a contradiction? A key factor in the myth is the fact that Hercules "strangled the two snakes" in his cradle, snakes that Hera had sent to kill him! Perhaps these two snakes, the two energies, were the key to his strength after all.

When he did die in the end, as we all are fated to, the gods accepted him on Mt. Olympus as an immortal, while Hera offered him her daughter, Hebe, to be his wife. The legends relating to this hero seem to tell us that Hercules, after taming the two universal energies in his cradle, obtained mythical powers, and—after having lived an adventurous, troublesome, and tumultuous life—chose Virtue, and earned, finally, eternal life and eternal youth as a result.

The Spartans—who were descendants of Hercules according to their mythology—used the symbol of the snakes extensively in their worship and to accompany them into battle. On the Spartan banner, the two snakes symbolize the Dioscouri, the two sons of Zeus, of whom one is mortal and the other is immortal (reminiscent of "form" and "infinity") (figure 4.6). Generally, representations of heroes and ancestors in ancient Sparta included a depiction of a curled up snake, symbolizing immortality and the heroic ideal. In another presentation, the Dioscouri are symbolized by two snakes wrapped up spirally around two amphoras (figure 4.7). Maybe it is not by chance, as we shall see, that the main temple in Sparta was the temple of "Standing" Artemis (Artemis Orthia).

In the legend of Hercules, the hero often misbehaved or lost his sanity, committed malevolent acts, and was forced to seek redemption. It seems that heroes had to be moral; otherwise insanity and failure were their punishments. In the Bhagavad Gita ("The Song of God"), dated around 1400 BCE, the avatar Krishna converses with the warrior Arjuna about the meaning of life. Krishna teaches him that a warrior must have a code of morals and be ready to fight and die for what is right. The *Iliad* also contains references to yin and yang and the noble behavior and morals of warriors. For example, in Rhapsody C, line 100, Hector stops the battle between the Achaeans and the Trojans in

Figure 4.5a, b. Neolithic representations from the Gilf Kebir caves, at the border between southwest Egypt and Libya. (Drawings by Kostas Dervenis.)

Figure 4.6. The Spartan banner, two snakes symbolizing the Dioscouri, seventh century BCE or earlier. (Drawing of an epitaph pillar at the Spartan Museum, by M. N. Todd and A. J. B. Wace in 1906.)

Figure 4.7. Spartan coin symbolizing the Dioscouri as two amphoras, each of them surrounded by a snake in a spiral coil.

order to propose a duel between Menelaos and Paris-Alexander. He holds his spear at the middle and approaches the mass of warriors, keeping the Trojans behind him. Hundreds of spears and arrows are aimed at him, but not one is shot.

"Let the Trojans and the Achaeans [Greeks] place their weapons on the earth, which feeds all living things, while Alexander and Ares-friend [warlike] Menelaos duel for Helen and her wealth," he said.

And Menelaos answered: "I think that now the Argeians [Greeks] and the Trojans may depart peacefully, as they have suffered enough because of my fight with Alexander. One of us will be killed, as decided by Fate, but you will all become friends. So, fetch a white ram and a black lamb for the sun and the moon, and we shall bring a third animal in Zeus's honor."*

The white ram was to be dedicated to the sun (yang) and the black lamb for the earth (yin), while Zeus's full name is Dias-Zeus, he who "couples the divided," he who connects yin and yang. The reference to the earth, "which feeds all living things," indicates they had a better-developed ecological awareness than we have today.

It should be noted that the ancient Greeks did not honor Ares (Mars), the god of war, but rather considered him a necessary evil. His holy bird was the vulture and destruction was his joy. Thus the adjective "Ares-friend" (Areiphilos), literally translated as "Ares's friend" and meaning warlike, used by Hector about Menelaos is a hidden insult. Ares is the god of destruction and the enemy of culture.

The goddess Athena, on the other hand, symbolizes the pure heart of the elite warrior, and she fights with spiritual and psychic strength. She wears armor and holds a spear, while at the same time she is the protector of culture and the arts. Athena is the goddess of warriors and heroes, those who protect society, and this is why she is called Proma-chos, meaning the one who "fights in front" (in the front line). It is not insignificant that Athena is a virgin—her purity symbolizes the power of the transformation of the sexual urge to esoteric spiritual power.

The sculptures of the Parthenon included a statue of the goddess in battle, vanquishing a giant. Snakes jump from her hands—a universal

*Homer, *The Iliad*, 3.95.

symbol, as we have seen, of esoteric power. At one point in the *Iliad*, Athena confronts Ares and beats him in battle. "Idiot!" she shouted. "Even now you still do not comprehend that I am beyond your powers, since you dare face me!" And so saying, she struck him on the back of the neck, paralyzing his limbs, and Ares falling took up seven acres of land, his hair filling with dust, his armor crashing like thunder on the earth."*

It is obvious that this excerpt is a description of a high standard of martial arts' expertise, since Athena beat Mars without any difficulty, hitting him on a point of his body that paralyzed him with one blow. This incident symbolizes the confrontation between the warrior elite on one side and barbaric brute force on the other: society's protector against the destroyer of culture.

## ATHENA AND MEDUSA: INGENIOUS FEMALE WISDOM

On Athena's shield, the head of Medusa is depicted, representing the chaotic powers of infinity, and indicating an important connection, one that is pertinent to our investigation. The name Medusa means "ingenious female wisdom" and corresponds in Sanskrit to the goddess Medha, in Egyptian to the goddess Met or Maat—it is obvious that the name, as well as the worship of "female wisdom," was spread worldwide. Medusa's worship came to Greece from Libya. In the Corfu Museum is the pediment of the temple of Artemis (585 BCE) where Artemis, another virgin goddess, is depicted in the form of Medusa. Medusa's abdomen bears the two snakes, familiar symbol of the entanglement of the two energies. Artemis, protector of animals, is a goddess with obvious shamanistic roots, as we have seen at the Akroteri cave.

Athena is the daughter of Zeus and Metis, the goddess of ingenious intuition, shrewdness, prudence, and premonitions that allow one to avoid a pitfall; she was also the goddess of hunting and fishing. In ancient times the term *dolos* (deceit, craftiness), attributed to Metis, did not have such a negative meaning as it does now. On the contrary, it corresponded to the same concept expressed by the word *doloma* (bait) in fishing and hunting. Metis is the craftiness that allows one with less

---

*Homer, *The Iliad,* F.405–410.

Figure 4.8. Pediment of the Artemis temple, Corfu Museum.

body strength or a poorer strategic position to win a battle. How can a fisherman catch a fish without bait? How can a hunter kill his prey if not with craftiness? How can a man with inferior physical attributes defeat a cave bear? Metis was that primitive goddess who allowed humans to prevail over more powerful opponents and natural dangers. She was the goddess of caves. It is worth noting that the name Metis has the same root as the word *metera*—"mother"—derived from the archaic root *MT,* which existed, as we have seen, internationally. In fact the English word "mother" derives from the same root.

In the *Iliad,* Ulysses is called *polymetis* for his craftiness, which led to the construction of the Trojan Horse. *Metis* refers to the possibility of maneuvers, of absorption, deflection, diversion, flexibility—what the Chinese would call yin.* It is apparent that the correlation between Metis and Potnia Theron (Mistress of the Animals), shamanism, and the caves is not accidental.

The displacement of Earth worship by the flamboyant Apollonian gods appears everywhere in the archaeological record as well as the mythological archives of Greece. Phoebus Apollo vanquished the Earth Dragon of Delphi and made his home his own. Zeus beat the proto-gods, the Titans, and buried them in the earth, choosing Olympus for his domicile. (Zeus's weapon was lightning, a symbol that appears worldwide in the mythological archives of the gods of the sky). However, Emperor Zeus was terrified of the prophecy uttered by the Titan Prometheus, according to which earthy Metis would give birth to a child who would dethrone him, so he swallowed her up while she was pregnant with Athena (an act symbolizing the alliance with and the absorption of the ancient power of the Goddess). Zeus gained the gift of premonition, the trembling in one's intestines, the "gut feeling" as we say today, because Metis was imprisoned inside his body.

However, one part of Metis could not be controlled, the part that was connected to the chaotic power that exists in the depths of the earth— the wild aspect of Medusa.† How could a reconciliation be achieved between the wild, chaotic, earthy force and the new gods of light and the Word? Only through peaceful forms of the deities. So, bronze-clad Athena, daughter of Metis, jumped out of Zeus's head. Later she helped Perseus to vanquish and kill Medusa but she also grabbed the head of the gorgon and put it on her shield.

The gorgon Medusa (the word *gorgo* means "shiny eyes") symbolizes the chaotic power of infinity, the same power that exists inside a black hole, where there is no time, shape, or form. Any average human who looks at it is petrified. To be able to control this power, one must be

---

*For those who practice the martial arts, *metis* is the *ju* in the word *jujutsu.*

†We believe that the relation between Metis and Medusa is the same as the relation between the peaceful and the wrathful depictions of Buddha in Tantric Buddhism today. For example, in Japanese Buddhism the Bodhisattva Fudo-Myoo (Acalanatha), a terrifying figure, is considered as the wrathful form of the central universal Buddha Vairocana; Buddhas take up a wrathful aspect in order to terrify the powers of evil.

extremely pure, with a purity equal to that of Athena and Artemis, both virgins. (This is the reason why Perseus needed to endure many trials before he could cut off Medusa's head.)

## FALLS FROM GRACE

The transformation of the sexual urge into celestial energy is a difficult and painful procedure, and several times heroes who were not always pure fell from divine grace and gave in to the pleasures of the flesh. A good example is Samson from the Old Testament. Samson was a Nazirite, that is, "he who renounces," and a holy warrior who fought against the Philistines during the early years of Israel (twelfth to tenth century BCE).

The Nazirites were zealots who renounced wine and took an oath never to cut their hair. These can all be understood as symbolizing their having sacrificed the pleasure of ejaculation in the name of God. Samson was a "kundalini hermit," a discipline that gave him his admirable strength. In Hebrew, his name is spelled *Shimson* and it means "the son of the sun"—in other words, "he who accumulates the solar spirit." The power of solar breath enabled Shimson to kill a lion with his bare hands, to move the gates of Gaza, to kill one thousand Philistines with a donkey's jaw, and so forth.

However, the sexual urge is a formidable opponent and Samson gave in to it not once but tens of times. His passion for Delilah, a Philistine woman allied with his enemies, brought him to his end. Her name in Hebrew is spelled *Dalila,* which simply means "desire." So, what this biblical myth tells us is that the son of the sun had a special passion for beautiful Philistine women, so much so that he gave in to his desires repeatedly, lost control, and sank into the pleasures of sexual love, losing his supernatural powers in the process, and thus falling prey to his enemies.

Even the first hero to preach about this heroic resistance to sexual lust had problems coping with sexuality. In 2700 BCE, the Babylonian Gilgamesh, divine king of Uruk with superhuman powers, insisted on sleeping with the wives and daughters of his subjects. Most likely, he went through the sexual act without orgasm. (Transformation of the sexual urge does not make a man moral. On the contrary, it makes him show his real nature. This is why it should be taught only to good people.) Gilgamesh overdid it and, in order to bring him back to order, the gods created Enkidu, who grew up in the desert, away from the temptations of the flesh. He protected animals from hunters, breaking up their traps and tearing their nets.

Enkidu's strength was unbelievable. He could beat whole armies. The inhabitants of Uruk were desperate and turned to Gilgamesh for help, and he found a solution immediately! "No problem," he told them. "Take a prostitute and ask her to wait near the fountain where he goes to drink water. When she sees him, let her show him her bare breasts and smile provocatively. He will fall head over heels for her, and after he finishes, he will be weak as a lamb." And so it happened. Poor Enkidu, after having sex, tried desperately to approach the gazelles he was guarding, but when they saw him so weak they ran away. Unhappy, he went back to where the competent young lady was contentedly brushing her hair. She finished him off with some flattery: "You are so handsome, Enkidu, you shine like a god! What are you doing all alone out here in the desert? Come back with me to the city of Uruk . . ." And so Enkidu followed her like a lamb, and later became clever Gilgamesh's right hand man. It is obvious from this story that he lost his divine power as soon as he gave in to sexual temptation.

These stories may be amusing, but they (especially when combined with the archaeological archives) also reveal that the practice of sexual temperance was spread all over the world in the Bronze Age, and that the strength of the divine warriors was attributed to this practice. The presence of the symbol of the two spirally entangled snakes (the breath, the chi or ki, yin and yang) is a decisive sign in all ancient societies. Possibly a minor "leftover" of these practices exists today among the wrestlers in India and Pakistan. These wrestlers, who are considered the best in the world and even invincible in contest, practice yoga and breathing exercises starting when they are quite young. Furthermore, their main concern is sexual temperance and the transformation of sexual energy into another, superior form (this practice is called *brahmacharya*). "The sperm," say the wrestlers, "is the substance of life and the source of any energy. A fighter must guard his sperm like a jeweler guards his most expensive diamonds."

An interesting guess is that the European knights of the Middle Ages, the Knights Templar, those formidable Crusade warriors, possibly used similar practices in their secret meetings. They certainly emphasized sexual abstention. They punished homosexuality by whipping and the guilty parties were expelled from the Brotherhood; they also punished heterosexual relations, though less severely—the guilty party would be demoted from his position temporarily and they would take away his responsibilities in the Brotherhood.

## MODERN MASTERY

Leaving the ancient years behind and with them the fossils of these ancient practices, let us return to present times. In addition to the symbolism of the spiral helix in the archaeological archives—which was most likely closely connected to the *mechanism* of these phenomena—it is useful to examine thoroughly, under the prism of modern science, the phenomena Professor Benson and his team recorded, and how can they be explained.

On the front wall of the Gouverneto Monastery, the monastery nearest to the Artemis cave, there is an amazing inscription, which is more reminiscent of Zen Buddhist dogma than that of the Orthodox Church: "Mind Decorates All Things and Is the Reason for All Being" (figure 4.9). This phrase is also reminiscent of Anaxagoras' philosophy, and indicates that ancient ideas influenced Christian Orthodoxy to a certain degree, in spite of the clergy's initial resistance.

Let us focus on the word *mind*. One part of our unconscious self is expressed through our autonomous nervous system and through our own cells. Each of our body's cells, through its microtubules, has the capacity for memory storage and for absorbing awareness. This raises the question: How can our physical integrity be maintained? Contrary to the theories of Descartes, the structure of our cells is neither permanent nor mechanical; the biology of our body is very close to quantum physics. Our bodies are in continuous incessant flow, cells die and get replaced every second. The pancreas, for example, changes all its cells every twenty-four hours, while the stomach needs three days for this. Our white blood cells are replaced every ten days, while 98 percent of the tissue of that most complex organ, the brain, is replaced every month. So, what keeps our form the same? Probably none other than a logistics program in our unconscious mind, a program that determines the form of our new cells while the old ones die.

Modern biochemistry maintains that this replacement is predetermined and controlled chemically through the proteins from our own

Figure 4.9. "Mind Decorates All Things and Is the Reason for All Being." Inscription over the gate of a chapel at Gouverneto Monastery.

genes. However, this theory cannot provide an explanation for the post-transplant phenomenon of recipients acquiring the preferences of their donors. Furthermore, the purely biochemical model, based on protein function, seems to have some problems concerning coherence and order in general. It would be interesting to suggest that protein function is nothing more than a natural procedure determined by the same afore-mentioned logistics software. If so, what would it mean to control this program?

We are microcosms in a macrocosm, and "Form and Infinity coexist within ourselves." Let us go back to the Tibetan monks who, exercising the gTummo yoga, basically control their autonomous nervous systems and the unconscious functions of all the cells of their bodies. This is determined by the observed high temperature of 115°F in their limbs, for the following reason: the brain cells of the human body suffer irre-versible damage and die when their temperature exceeds 108°F. This biochemical restriction could mean two things: either the monks raise the temperature only on the outside of the body, that is, the limbs and the skin, and protect the inside organs and the brain by keeping their temperature lower, or their temperature goes up to 115 degrees through-out the body. In the first case, the monks control their body metabolism locally, which means that they can exert control over the autonomous programming at the cellular level: they choose to increase the tempera-ture of their limbs and the skin, while the inside temperature of their organs remains steady at a lower temperature. In the second case, they control the biochemistry of their brain cells, making them invulnerable to the increased temperature, which is even more amazing. Undoubtedly, in either case, they control the autonomous functions of the nervous system and the cells locally.*

How can the monks do this? Could it be that our cells have memory and that the spiral helix model plays its part in this exercise, as the monks maintain? And if this cellular control were expressed in another form, instead of temperature control, what would be the powers of its owner? Could this provide an explanation for all the stories about the amazing powers of great teachers of the East, in our times?†

One of the authors of this book has had personal experiences that support the connection between the control of sexual energy and extraordinary abilities. This author was a renunciant for eight years, during which he followed a steady course of transforming sexual energy, which originated in the Chinese tradition of *neikung,* "esoteric energy."‡ During this period, there were many changes in his physical condition and consciousness. In his palms, for example, "stigmata" appeared (a little above the center of the palm); these were local hyperemias, which, according to the doctors, "looked like burns"; the same thing happened to the ends of his fingers and the spaces in between them (figure 4.10). Furthermore, he became inexplicably strong for his physical shape and structure and considering the short amount of time he devoted to physical exercise. The phenomenon of increased temperature presented with gTummo was apparent, up to the point where he was comfortable in the snow wearing just a T-shirt.

In addition, a low power electrical current was felt both by the author and his students during practice, coming from the area of *dantien,* the energy center at the lower abdomen. He and his students both experienced changes in consciousness as well: telepathic and prognosis phenomena were frequent, as were phenomena of remote viewing. From the negative side, there were also altered states of consciousness, where the borders between reality and imagination could not be defined clearly.

---

*We remind the reader that the discovery of spiral microtubules in our cells started with the simple question, "How are mental signals (hunger, attack, defense, escape) transferred in single cell organisms that lack a nervous system?"

†Or is there something even more peculiar going on that is still beyond our powers to perceive?

‡The author still continues to practice, but under a less severe discipline.

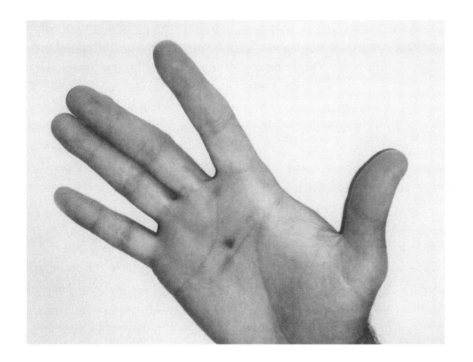

Figure 4.10. Local hyperemia in the palm as a result of esoteric exercise.

Also from a negative side, we learned that 60 percent of the Chinese trainees in the most difficult practices (not those practiced by beginners) of *neikung,* in a specific age group, had complications, some of them leading to death. Most of the complications were related to hypertension, which occurred as a result of the neikung exercise, which should have been monitored and controlled by the student with other practices or aerobics. (Specifically, death was attributed to stroke, heart problems, and kidney failure, all as a consequence of hypertension.) These side effects probably occurred because this strenuous discipline was meant to be a monastic practice, while the Chinese trainees attempted to adhere to the discipline in the framework of an everyday lifestyle in contemporary society, something very difficult, if not impossible, to do.

If the results of the breathing and meditation practices experienced by the author are compared to the mythological and archaeological archives, one can see that they are reflected absolutely. The phenomenon of increased temperature and the "burns" in the palms, as well as the unnatural strength, could be attributed to the Apollonian element, to the solar or celestial energy, the cultivation and spread of which is the foundation of these practices (the enhancement of "form"). On the other hand, the phenomena of telepathy, intuition, and premonition could be attributed to the development of *metis*, an outcome of the second principle of these practices, the accumulation and distribution of chaotic or chthonian energy (the enhancement of "infinity"). The "altered states of consciousness" are the face of Medusa, which petrifies the unsuspecting. In order for a renunciant to confront her, he must have heroic strength and purity, as well as the correct technical knowledge. It seems safe to conclude that these breathing and meditation practices correspond to the path that goddess Athena symbolized for the ancient ancestors of the Greeks.

These results observed are not hard to explain based on modern physics. As mentioned earlier, two forces constitute the natural form of space-time: one of them we shall call *light* (coming from the stars) and the other one we shall call *chaos* (coming from gravity and dark matter). It is not possible that such a confrontation would prevail in the universe and not be reflected within our own body, within our consciousness.

The "collective unconscious" is a term introduced by the great psychiatrist Carl Gustav Jung to describe that part of our mind shared by the entire human race, which is reflected in our brain anatomy. We have described the structure of space-time in the universe already. If our consciousness follows the same structure, as Jung believed, then it can be symbolized with the following model:

This configuration, corresponding to the cosmic structure observed by astrophysics, would explain many of the so-called paraphysical and parapsychological phenomena. One part of our mind, our unconscious

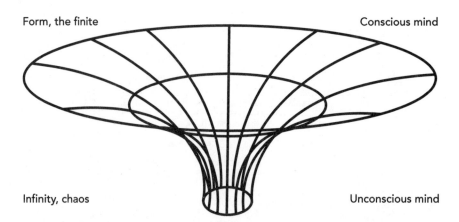

Figure 4.11. The structure of consciousness

Form, the finite — Conscious mind

Infinity, chaos — Unconscious mind

210
THE INNER PATH

self, manifests in the autonomous nervous system of our body, while it continues inside our own cells. (In the light of Jung's collective unconscious, the aforementioned structure demonstrates the possibility that in infinite space our consciousness is connected, that we are all like the fingers of one hand, connected at the palm: we believe that we are independent beings, but in effect one part of our self is shared in common with everyone else.)

## THE PATH OF THE WARRIOR

Returning to ancient mythology, let us take up the Medusa theme. A universally accepted theory, based on archaeological and literary archives, is that by the end of the third millennium and the beginning of the second millennium BCE, the existing spiritual and political hierarchy and authority of women/shamans, which had existed for tens of millennia, passed on to men/warriors in each tribe. This transfer of authority was a global phenomenon. It is not accidental that there was also a global change in the worship of the gods of thunder and the sky, replacing the existing worship of earth deities.

The myth of Perseus can be seen as a powerful symbol of this transfer of spiritual and cultural authority from women to men. It is obvious that women/shamans were using the power of the earth exclusively, demonstrated by the archaeological evidence of the sacred caves. Perhaps, due to their nature, women had better access to the plane of chthonic powers than men did (such a suggestion would not be illogical).

Medusa's formidable gaze petrified those men who looked at her: perhaps the "ingenious female wisdom" was a state of consciousness that could not be tolerated by the male mind's structure. However, the time came when, after many experiments and many failures (which probably led to death, illness, and insanity), men/warriors realized they could use both energies of the universe entangled together through the practice of sexual temperance. The worldwide symbolism of the gods of thunder may be significant in the methodology of the transformation of sexual energy. Athena symbolizes the reconciliation of the two tendencies, the gods of the bright sky and the earthy chaos, Athena who controls both the power of the thunder and the formidable gaze of the gorgon through her purity and her warrior's virtue.

Hercules strangled the two snakes, becoming Hera's glory and Zeus's

Figure 4.12. Perseus kills the Medusa. Neoclassical work by Canova, ca. 1804, Vatican Museum.

son, and authority changed hands from women to men. Virtue, respect for culture, the position of Promachos (one who "fights up front," protecting society), sexual temperance, and the transformation of this basic vital energy into a superior spiritual form—this has been and will be the esoteric path of true warriors, from prehistoric times until today.

# EPILOGUE

In the past few years, there has been a lot of commotion over the terms *submission grappling* (or *wrestling*) and *submission fighting* (or *mixed martial arts*). All those involved with martial arts today strive to acquire some knowledge of submission and control holds, as well as the strategy and tactics of the great athletes and fighters competing in mixed martial arts contests. Most people believe that submission fighting is a contemporary form of combat, an innovation, with the assumption that—although it is based on more traditional combat systems (like jiu jitsu)—the system as it appears today is absolutely modern and new. Some people who have a greater knowledge of the evolution of combat sports in the twentieth century believe that submission wrestling is just a more refined type of judo. We hope this book makes it clear that in truth, it is the other way around: submission wrestling and submission fighting are combat sports that have been in existence since societies were fully organized millennia ago. The technical knowledge involved with staging a bloodless contest was developed over thousands of years by various peoples around the world, and was glorified in ancient Olympia by the combat sport of pankration. That having been said, we also hope that we have made it clear that martial arts and combat sports are two very separate things, each with their independent history and goals.

An athlete who participates in both the martial arts and combat sports introduces himself to a means of gaining mental and physical health that is not to be found in any other discipline. Study and exercise in the martial arts is never ending. Experience gained this way can be most important in our lives, as we rediscover ourselves continuously, define our limitations, and achieve our aims. And of course all of the above have a positive influence on our selves in the end. What is better for our psyche than holding up a mirror to our inner selves and knowing exactly what we look like? It is therefore important for an athlete to know what he is doing, both on a technical level as well as in a historical context. We believe that it is useful to know that pankration, as it is developing today, is the same combat sport that very important men, warriors, combative athletes, scientists, and philosophers have been practicing for thousands of years in the history of humankind. We hope this book provides some direction for those people who have lost their way among the hundreds of different martial art styles popular today—in the end, it is the essence of things that is important. Seek that essence, and you'll be fine.

# ANCIENT GREEK PAMMACHON AND THE ROOTS OF ZEN

The friezes on the Parthenon pediments, the temple of Epicurean Apollo, the temple of Olympian Zeus, and so many others, which depict a martial art very similar to Japanese jujutsu or Okinawan karate, raise the question of whether there is a connection between the ancient Greek martial art we shall call pammachon (to differentiate it from the combat sport of pankration) and the Shaolin kung fu of the Zen Patriarch Bodhidharma, the origin of many of the Eastern martial arts forms. At the beginning of the twentieth century (1905), Japanese jujutsu instructors visiting the West admitted that the aforementioned sculptures resembled their martial art.* Perhaps this is what led to the overeager declaration that "pankration was passed on to the Indians by Alexander, and from there on to the Chinese, and that's how karate was developed," which has been broadcast by those of Greek origin who have been promoting *pankration* in this generation. We wish that things were so simple. In this brief essay, we will try to outline the historical difficulties involved with tracing such a cultural interaction, and suggest a path by which the Greeks could have indeed influenced the martial arts of the East—or not.

---

*S. K. Uyenishi, *The Text-Book of Ju-Jutsu as Practiced in Japan* (London: Health and Strength, 1905).

There are written reports in China referring to the martial arts dating from 1000 BCE and archaeological evidence from 250 BCE, which make it obvious that the Chinese had developed martial arts long before the possibility of cultural transfer through Alexander's conquests. Furthermore, this ethnocentric approach does not take into consideration the activities of the Persians, the Indians, the Assyrians, the Sumerians, the Hittites, and so many other peoples, all of whom obviously knew and practiced martial arts, long before coming into contact with Greek influence.

It is clear that the Greek army's successes during the Persian war and Alexander's conquests was due to their superior military tactics (the armed phalanx, which their enemies did not know how to confront effectively), their advanced metallurgy (the success of their armor was very commendable, especially given the means available then), and the combat techniques they had developed, which corresponded well to their military tactics. This does not mean that other nations had not developed martial arts! In fact, there is an inscription on the tomb of Darius I, which shows that the king was boasting about his capabilities in the martial arts. This inscription—in addition to providing evidence of the existence of martial arts in Persia—proves that they were so important for their society that they provided a basis for boasting:

> This indeed is my activity. Inasmuch as my body has the strength, as battle-fighter I am a good battle-fighter. . . . Trained am I both with hands and with feet. As a horseman, I am a good horseman. As a bowman I am a good bowman both afoot and on horseback. As a spearman I am a good spearman both afoot and on horseback. And the skills which Ahuramazda has bestowed upon me and I have the strength to use them—by the favor of Ahuramazda what has been done by me, I have done with those skills that Ahuramazda bestowed upon me.*

We must recall the example of Dioxippos in his duel against Koragos, a proof that Macedonians generally did not have a great appreciation for pankration—in fact, it appears they did not believe in it. It has been recorded that Alexander was against combat sports as a training method for soldiers. The standpoint therefore that "Alexander brought pankra-

---

*John Boardman, *Persia and the West* (London: Thames and Hudson, 2000), 220.

tion to the Hindus" must be rejected by the reader, if for no other reason than it appears Alexander himself had actually rejected pankration! The lack of any evidence for this case, combined with the plethora of proof against it, is the reason why not one bona fide historian has taken this assertion seriously. However, Alexander's path of conquest and the earlier Greek victories in the Persian wars do verify that the close-quarter combat tactics of the Near Eastern people *were* inferior to those of the classical Greeks, beginning roughly circa the fifth century BCE, simply because their leaders preferred distant engagement of their enemies (i.e., missile warfare) to close-quarter engagement (while, on the other hand, in the second century BCE the martial arts of the Greeks were inferior to those of the Romans, who excelled at close-quarter combat as well as military strategy).

In 326 BCE, Alexander penetrated into India, using a military strategy developed by his father, that is to say, a tight phalanx with soldiers carrying *sarissas* (long heavy pikes), with cavalry support for their flanks. The soldiers of Alexander worked as one unit, emphasizing correct positioning and the strength of the erect body. The *sarissa* was held in both hands; therefore the soldier could only strike using the power of his waist and legs. This technique has obvious correlation with the techniques of classical karate and classical jujutsu. This makes it easy to fall into the trap of thinking that karate is the same art used by Alexander, and that the Greeks had created it.

Although we knew that all the peoples in the world had developed martial arts since the Bronze Age, we had hoped that the techniques of fighting while wearing heavy armor would provide some means for tracking the spread of Greek martial arts. Unfortunately, this does not apply. The Chinese had also developed the use of heavy armor as early as the Zhou dynasty, in the eleventh century BCE. Their armor consisted of hundreds of bronze plates, sewn onto a leather gown, so as not to restrict the movement of the warrior. The evolution of this bronze armor was brought to light by the archaeological discovery of armor dated to 154 BCE from the Chu kingdom, consisting of 2,000 pieces of steel with six eyes on each piece, so that they could be linked together, like "fish scales." This armor, in spite of its flexibility, together with a shield and helmet, was extremely heavy, so that the soldier wearing it needed to know the right technique in order to move freely when engaged in combat.

In other words, the existence of similarities in kinesiology in the ancient West and the ancient East does not necessarily mean anything, because: 1) the kinesiology of the human body is a given and nothing has changed in the past 40,000 years, as far as we know; 2) the spread of martial arts, as we have seen elsewhere in this book, must be placed during the Neolithic Age; and 3) all these arts are based on the movement of a warrior while wearing heavy armor. Consequentially, they would of necessity be similar to each other—any nation that developed combat techniques based on heavy armor had to consider the same principles. So any link that could exist between the ancient Greek martial arts and those of the East must be looked for elsewhere.

## THE BUDDHIST CONNECTION

It is still possible that the Greeks did have an influence on the martial arts of the East; it is just that the right path has to be established. We believe that this path may be through the Buddhist religion. Historical events and archaeological archives may offer a clue regarding cultural exchange between Greece and China concerning the martial arts. Those readers who are strict rationalists could accuse us of searching for a correlating link for personal reasons, given that we are Greek. And they would not be wrong. In spite of this, let us proceed, making clear that we shall base our conclusions on six specific, related assumptions:

1. As we have seen repeatedly so far, the development of the martial arts was a universal phenomenon during the Bronze Age, and a characteristic trait of warriors, devotees of the sacred duel.

The first archaeological evidence of martial arts comes from Egypt and Mesopotamia. We have already presented and examined the wall drawings at the Egyptian tombs of Beni Hasan dating from 2000 BCE, which depict refined techniques of combat sports, mainly submission wrestling. There are also depictions from Mesopotamia, from the same time period, which depict a middle block to a punch, a move that many karate athletes would recognize today. The fact is that up to the year 2000 BCE, both martial arts and combat sports were spread throughout the world, from China to England. From that period on, they developed according to their particular cultural, climatological, and environmental conditions, as well as the military needs and particularities of each nation.

In China they evolved into the Taoist martial arts by around 800 B.C.E. In India they took the form of the martial art of *kalari payat,* the sacred duel and martial art of vajramushti, and the folk dances of *nata* dance. In the Middle East we can say with certainty that in the year 1000 BCE there was no difference between the martial arts of the Egyptians, the Assyrians, the Hittites, and the Greeks. The martial art of the Greeks started to differentiate from the rest circa the eighth century BCE, which, as we have seen, was due to the adoption of heavy armor and particular tactics.

2. The martial arts (pammachon) of the Greeks during the classical age were undoubtedly and definitively connected to the worship of the Olympian Gods.

The fact that the Parthenon sculptures and those of the temple of Apollo in Bassai represent scenes of the martial arts is the best proof for this statement. Besides, it is quite obvious. The ancient Greeks were warriors. It is not accidental that their martial art had theological connotations. Think again of the heavily armed Athena, a goddess who combined martial arts with wisdom and virtue. And remember, too, that all the wrestling, boxing, and pankration contests took place in honor of the gods (Olympia, Nemea, Isthmia) at religious festivals, while all classical competitions in general (track athletics, discus, and the javelin throw) were products of training for battle. The relation between gods and heroes is obvious in all myths, as well as in the *Iliad* and the *Odyssey.* The connection between pammachon and worship of the gods is significant because, as we shall see below, this had a specific influence on Buddhism.

3. The main contribution of Alexander the Great can be summarized in one phrase: he tore down the walls between nations and forced the citizens of various states to talk to each other face to face. The Persians started to get along with the Greeks, the Indians began talking to the Romans, the Parthians found they had things in common with the Egyptians. With the end of the Hellenistic age and the emergence of the Roman domination, the Silk Road was created, through which products were transferred from Luoyang in China to far away England and vice versa. Greek sailors of the age were sailing from the Red Sea through Indonesia to coastal Canton! Alexander was the Internet of

his era. No nation remained uninfluenced by the intense changes and interactions during the Hellenistic era. Not even the Greeks. Along with various other cultural influences, there was a broad exchange of religious and spiritual beliefs. The Greeks were fascinated by the mysticism and the bioenergy exercises of the Hindus. An example is Alexander himself and his relationship with the Hindu gymnosophist guru Kalanos. Many Greeks became Buddhists, and this is the main point of our theme.

The first Greek Buddhist was a monk in 240 BCE. One hundred years later, when Menander was the king, Buddhist documents refer to 10,000 Greek Buddhist monks. In the years 160–145 BCE, Menander reigned in Sakala of Bactria. His kingdom covered south Afghanistan and the entire Punjab up to the Ganges, including the Rajasthan desert. A loyal Buddhist, he filled India with Buddhist monuments and generally supported their philosophy. When he died, he was pronounced a saint of Buddhism, and his ashes were considered sacred treasures. During his reign the *ksatriya* warriors of India became friendly with the Greek soldiers and even enrolled the Greeks in their caste. It is no coincidence that the god of Hindu warriors, Indra *vajrahasta* ("he who holds the thunder") resembles Zeus, and that this association is primal, going back to the overthrow of the Earth Mother by the sky gods mentioned in previous chapters.

The last Hellenistic kingdoms of Bactria expired in 30 BCE, but the cultural influence of Alexander's conquering expedition went on for almost 1,000 years. In the first century CE, the Kusans, a Mongolian tribe from Turkestan in China, conquered Bactria. The Parthians and the Sakkas were expelled. For some reason, the Greeks remained. (This would demonstrate Greek-Turkish friendship circa the first century CE? Amusing.) An amazing civilization was created, where the Greek alphabet was adopted for the Kusan language and deities had common Greek and Kusan characteristics. In 40 CE, King Kanishka of the Kusans became the next Dharmaraja after Asoka and Menander, protecting and spreading Buddhism.

There was a great transfer of ideas as well as merchandise along the Silk Road. In the first century, the Greek Apollonius of Tyana traveled to India where he studied the secrets of Tantric yoga. It is recorded that the Roman Emperor Marcus Aurelius Antoninus sent an ambassador to China during his reign. And, in 353 CE, despite the growing enforcement of Christianity by the Roman conquerors, the most popular religions in Greece were, in addition to the worship of the Olympian Gods, the worship of the Persian god Mithra and Egyptian goddess Isis.

There was as much Greek influence in the East as there was Eastern influence in the West. Gandhara, a Bactrian town, produced the first Buddhist sculptures in the Greek manner. In the Gandhara sculptures that survive today, the Bodhisattva Vajrapani ("thunder in hand") is presented in Zeus's form. Many historians maintain that the Greeks of Bactria are responsible for the development of Mahayana Buddhism—significantly, Athena, holding lightning in her hand as an upraised spear, was the main deity in Bactria. We must not underestimate Persia's importance as a mediator between these two poles. For example, when the seventh century CE Buddhist king of Tibet, Srongtsan Gampo, challenged doctors from all over the world to a "duel," the Persian doctor Galenos (Galen) practicing Greek medicine emerged as the victor (and he was obviously a Greek from Persia). Persian influence was particularly important between the first and the seventh century CE. When the conquering Roman emperor Justinian, who spoke only Latin and not Greek, closed Plato's Academy for good, in 529, the "seven wise men of Athens" found refuge in the court of the Persian king Khosroe. There are also clear indications that the Tibetan Bön religion, which influenced Tibetan Buddhism as well, is most likely of Persian origin.*

Another Persian religion, Manichaeism, is significant in this respect. In 216 CE, Manichaeus was born in Persia. Half Parthian, he created a new dogma in the gnostic model, which borrowed elements from all existing religions of the time. This new religion, which promoted the chance of spontaneous individual enlightenment (just like Zen), spread worldwide with such passion that Manichaeus was captured, tortured, and killed in Persia in his old age. There is evidence that Manichaeism had a deep influence on Mahayana Buddhism (after having absorbed elements from it), and contributed to the creation of the method of "sudden enlightenment" attributed to Bodhidharma, which is called *dhyana* in Sanskrit, *ch'an* in Chinese, *dzogcen* in Tibetan, and *zen* in Japanese. It would take too long to theologically examine the how's and why's of this statement in this brief appendix. Suffice it to say that Manichaeism

---

*Charles Allen, *The Search for Shangri-La* (London: Abacus, 2000).

connected Gnostic Christianity with Zoroastrianism and Buddhism and that it spread worldwide very quickly. In the West, for example, it created the heresies of the "Cathars" and the "Bogomiles," which the respective "Orthodox" Christian emperors were only able to wipe out after bloody campaigns. The Manichaeist religion, with its flexible belief system and its elimination of the clergy, spread easily among warriors, which is a significant observation for our study.

4. Since its first appearance in history, Buddhism has been connected with the martial arts. Sakyamuni Buddha, as a prince and member of the Hindu *ksatriya* warrior caste, was trained in the martial arts, including vajramushti, from a young age. The art of vajramushti ("thunder in the hand") is very interesting for two reasons:

a) It has been preserved until recently (the 1950s) as an annual "non-fatal" duel (it is hardly bloodless, however) at certain Hindu religious festivities, where two opponents fight wearing iron fists with pointed ends on their right hands, just like the Roman cestus. The purpose of this duel, in which all types of fighting are allowed, is the submission of the opponent and the control of his weapon, but not his injury. It is a dangerous form of submission fighting, perhaps in a more primitive form than pankration. The vajramushti ritual is reminiscent of the 2000 BCE Egyptian stick fights in honor of god Horus, indicating that vajra-mushti is probably ancient. Most likely, vajramushti is a ritual that has remained intact in India from the Bronze Age due to the caste system and the general emphasis of the East on maintaining the rituals of the past. It is obvious that vajramushti is an archaic form of close-quarter combat and its ritual confrontation undoubtedly symbolizes the clash between two men armed with knives.

b) Due to its connection with religious festivals it is obvious that it is a ritualistic combative art whose origins are related to ancient spiritual beliefs.

All martial arts, at their higher level, are characterized by breathing and kinesiological particularities, which aim at the distribution of bioenergy. For example, the Taoist martial arts, Indian kalari payat, and Japanese jujutsu are each individually characterized by specific types of breathing and styles of movement. As we have seen, it is likely that pammachon had a similar set of breathing exercises aimed at controlling and using bioenergy, which the Greeks called *pneuma*.

In the third century BCE, the Greeks went to India. The Hindus respected them for their culture as well as for their fighting spirit. One proof of this is that among all other "barbarians," only the Greeks were considered "humans" by the orthodox Hindus, who classified the Javanas (their name for the Greeks) in the *ksatriya* warrior caste. The interaction between Greek religion and philosophy and Buddhism created the Greco-Buddhist art of Gandhara and Mahayana Buddhism. We remind the reader that Greek *pammachon* was intimately tied to the old Olympian religion.

All of these factors lead us to this daring conclusion: along with Greek sculpture and philosophy, Buddhists absorbed *pammachon,* as the Greeks of that area became Buddhists, offering to their new religion, together with their sculpture and architecture, their martial art.

One of the basic changes that Buddhism imposed on the breathing-bioenergetical exercises of Hindu yoga was the transfer of emphasis from the gradual opening of the seventy-two chakras of the human entity to the exclusive preoccupation with the seven basic chakras on the central energy channel. (This approach has been extensively developed in books on Tantric Buddhism in the English language, so there is no reason to delve deeply into this subject here, as a brief reference should suffice.) Pammachon, due to its kinesiology, fit perfectly with the requirements of the breathing exercises of Buddhism in that era. (The center of gravity of a person wearing heavy armor is transferred higher, which calls for a special manner of moving and a special kind of abdominal breathing—especially when that person is wearing an inflexible breastplate, as the Greeks did.)

In this book then, we will support the premise that the Greek emphasis on upright close-quarter combat tactics, deriving from the phalanx and heavy armor, as well as the necessity of abdominal breathing while wearing such armor, clearly influenced the martial arts of the Indian warrior caste, as the techniques of pammachon were adopted by the aristocrats of India, who had become Buddhists. The ksatriya caste incorporated the methods of pammachon into their own art of *vajramushti.** Together with Greek sculpture and architecture, in other words,

---

*I mention *vajramushti* rather than *kalari payat* because the later seems far more tied to Hinduism than to Buddhism, and is hence less relevant to the historic progression we are proposing here.

Buddhists also absorbed pammachon, modifying and refining their own martial art in turn, as more and more Greeks became Buddhists.

5. We must point out the crucial importance of the Silk Road once again, which, based on the impetus of the Roman empire, connected the Mediterranean with China, beginning in the first century BCE. There are even indications that there was a Roman populace in China back in 50 BCE! To point out the complexity of that time, it is useful to refer to the possibility of the existence of this settlement, even though there is little concrete evidence for it, as we are more interested in it as an example than as an established fact.

In 1955 an American scholar from Oxford, Homer Hasenpflug Dubs, expressed the theory that there was a Roman town in China in the first century BCE. He found, in a cadastre of that time, a reference to a town called Liqian in west China. In the Chinese language of that era, Liqian was the name used for Rome. Furthermore, the Chinese of the Han dynasty used to name cities in their territory after the state the foreign inhabitants came from, whether these were prisoners or colonists. The problem is how the Romans in question could have gotten to China, since between Rome and China were the Parthians, fanatic enemies of both.

In searching for an answer Dubs turned to the ancient texts of both China and Rome. Plutarch reports that in 53 BCE, 42,000 Roman legionaries under the command of general Marcus Licinius Crassus left Rome to go to Asia and fight against the Parthians, whose kingdom then extended from today's Syria to Pakistan, with Iraq and Iran included. The Roman legion was decimated by the Parthians in the battle of Carrhae, by the border of today's Turkey and Syria. Crassus was beheaded and, according to Plinius, 10,000 Roman soldiers were captured and transferred to central Asia.

Dubs believed that an unknown number of Roman soldiers managed to escape from the Parthians and traverse the three hundred some miles from their prison to the border of the Huns in central Asia, given that the Huns were also enemies of the Parthians. There, they became mercenaries in the service of Jzh-Jzh, the chief of the Huns, who ruled over all of what today is Mongolia. Jzh-Jzh attempted many invasions against China, until he was finally defeated in Taskende in 36 BCE. In this battle, however, one unit of mercenaries in the service of Jzh-Jzh fought "with their shields in line like fish scales" (as a Chinese historical document of the time mentions), a tactic which, according to Dubs, refers to the Roman formation *testudo*, which has never appeared historically anywhere else but in the Roman army.

Furthermore, Jzh-Jzh's fort was encircled by a double protective fortification of wooden posts, a method used only by the Romans at the time. The Roman mercenaries were defeated again,* and 145 of the survivors were transferred to an area in west China, where they were offered their freedom in exchange for residing there as border guards in Gansu territory.

The small town they built was called Liqian in their honor. In the year 9 CE the Emperor Wang Mang changed its name temporarily to Jie-Lu, meaning "prisoners captured during the siege of a city," one additional indication that this is a reference to the town of the 145 prisoners. Unfortunately, there is no concrete archaeological evidence to prove Dubs's theory other than the aforementioned indications, although in the probable location of the ancient town, a wall was found from that time period, as well as a basin of Roman design, a water pot, and a Chinese helmet with the inscription "one of those who surrendered."

Any archaeologist, of course, would expect more concrete evidence,† but that is unlikely to come to light, since no captured army would be allowed to keep their own weapons (which became war trophies) and no politician would allow them cultural artifacts (or even their own native clothes), which they could use in order to escape. We know that Liqian existed up to 746 CE, when it was conquered and destroyed by the Tibetans. Various studies of the DNA of today's natives of the area, who have red hair and light colored eyes, show that they have a considerable percentage of European genes (which may also be due to the fact that this area was on the Silk Road).

Regardless of whether the above example carries any weight or not, we can be sure of two things:

a) It is clear that the Romans knew well what was going on in China in those days (and vice versa), since in the first century BCE there was already a Chinese name for Rome and in 166 CE the Roman emperor Marcus Aurelius Antoninus officially sent an ambassador to

---

*With bow and arrow, as they were defeated by the Parthians earlier.

†And counter-indications to the theory do exist.

China (although the Chinese themselves reached only as far west as Babylon).

b) Taking into consideration this long-lasting contact, it is certain that the Chinese had the opportunity to examine and evaluate the military methods as well as the martial arts and skills of the Romans. They surely knew that the Romans had conquered the Mediterranean and a large part of Europe and that they had had confrontations with their common enemy, the Parthians. It is interesting that the short sword of the first century BCE of western China, the *duan jian,* had approximately the same size as the Roman *gladius,** which supports the suggestion that the Chinese may have been interested in evaluating Roman close-quarter combat techniques.

These findings make it clear that the Hellenistic kingdoms in India were not the only sources of cultural exchange between East and West during this time period (although the Hellenistic kingdoms *were* a major factor in the creation of the Silk Road). How easily we forget that the Huns—who were a tribe (the Xiongnu) in northwest China in the second century BCE—reached the suburbs of Rome in the fourth century CE!

6. And so we come to the fifth century CE, in the midst of formidable changes, wars, and cultural interactions, and to the case of *Bodhidharma.* From the first century CE on, the spread of the varying sects and dogmas of Buddhism had been taking place in China. This dissemination was not easy; it took great effort and there were a lot of counter-reactions (since the interests of local religions were threatened). However, in 472 CE there are written testimonies from Buddhist monks in China, referring to the method of *dhyana,* which was later to become known as Ch'an (Zen). The Shaolin temple was built in 495 CE in the Sung Mountains in Hunan Province (the name of the temple means "young forest" and refers to the forest in northern India where the Buddha chose to die). It is certain that the creation of this temple contributed to some political scheme of that time. For example, in 535 CE, Mahayana Buddhism was established as the official state religion in the kingdom of the Sylla Dynasty in Korea, a clear political move, since

---

*Which does not mean, for God's sake, that they took it from the Romans! We refer to this particular sword only because the fact that it is the same size and shape naturally indicates comparable fighting tactics.

seven years earlier an aristocrat had been executed because he was a Buddhist! In 535 though, the Korean aristocracy decided to push the women-shamans of the indigenous religion out of the royal court by using State conversion to Buddhism as their official excuse. It is highly probable that events in China followed the same course.

In 530 CE, then, Buddhism was well established in China, in spite of the reactions of the local Taoist priests. And so we come to the case of Bodhidharma. To begin with, was there a historic Bodhidharma? His name means "He who brings the Wisdom-Method." Most researchers in the West maintain today that Bodhidharma was not a real person, and that this name was a creation of popular legend, given to various Buddhist missionaries who had crossed the borders of China. The same type of skeptics, however, maintain that Homer was not a real person either, and that his epic sagas are simply a collective synthesis of older works of lesser poets.

Nonsense.

Life has proven that genius is a privilege of the few, and that mediocrity always pursues it, in a relentless effort to either absorb it or destroy it. In spite of numerous efforts of competitors, in the end there was only one Mozart, one Picasso, one Einstein. History has shown us that in critical situations, major events and their outcomes depend on the efforts and decisions of only one person. Hannibal was one such person, and so was Bodhidharma. The same type of people who doubt Bodhidharma's historic existence today were for centuries dubious about the existence of Troy, until a German merchant beat them at their own game. Besides, as we have already confirmed, the spread of Buddhism throughout Asia took place in times of intense political conflict, warfare, and intercultural pressure. A strong personality is required under such circumstances; a person having to confront such adversities needs the heart of a warrior, not the meekness of a monk. The political controversy surrounding Buddhism's spread in China must have been quite dangerous, given that the country had been in a state of civil war for centuries. The myth reports that Bodhidharma met with Emperor Wu Di of the Liang dynasty in the town of Nanching. China had been divided into various small states and this meeting most certainly had a political character and expediency. The two men did not reach an agreement and, displeased, Bodhidharma left Nanching to go to the Shaolin temple.

Bodhidharma had blue eyes and was very likely a Persian rather than a pureblooded Indian. He was a prince of a small tribe in Kancipura, south India. We propose that this royal family had descended from Persians who fled the persecution of followers of Manichaeism after the execution of Mani in 274 CE.* Bodhidharma lived at a time when war was prevalent, as the Huns had invaded India and were looting and pillaging to the north. As a prince, he would have been a member of the warrior caste and would naturally have started learning the martial arts at a very young age, much like the Buddha himself. We believe that he became a follower of Buddhism *specifically* because he was trained in the amalgam of vajramushti and pammachon we referred to earlier. He studied Buddhism under a teacher who had nothing to do with the martial arts or with the Ch'an dogma. This teacher's name was Prajnatara, and he belonged to the Sarvastivada dogma, one of the first Mahayana schools.

The conditions outlined above support our contention that the Ch'an school, and its combination with the martial arts, were clearly *Bodhidharma's innovation, based on the Manichean past of his family and his own training in vajramushti.* When he went to the Shaolin temple in China and reached the height of his powers, he established a system of sudden enlightenment based on his own background in *ksatriya*-derived yogic breathing and on the *dhyana* meditation he studied as a Mahayana Buddhist exercise. The legend tells us that he taught the monks two practices: one meant to strengthen the organism and the physical body *(yi gin ching)* and one to transform sexual energy into spiritual power *(shi sui ching)*. He taught the Buddhist asceticism of the *Lankavatara Sutra*. Clearly, what he wanted to pass on to the monks was the concept of warrior virtue and how it could be combined with Buddhism.

The Chinese historian Chang-ning (919–1001, of the Sung Dynasty) reports clearly and positively on Bodhidharma, commenting on his role in the extinction of the garrulous literature then prevalent in Chinese Buddhism. "Address the human Mind, see your own true Nature and

---

*Manichaeists were expelled from Persia by the supporters of the official state religion (Zoroastrianism at this time) and the legend of Bodhidharma explicitly states that he had blue eyes, something that would be impossible if he was of Dravidian stock. Of course, this brings up the question as to what type of Aryan/Dravidian racial mix held sway in southern India during the sixth century CE, but it is probably safe to say that there were not many blue-eyed Indians in southern India during this time.

become Buddhas, do not focus on words, phrases, or symbols"—this is how Chang-ning records Bodhidharma's words. This teaching, combined with the knightly virtue prevalent in Bodhidharma's legend, indicates the heart and methods of a warrior, not the dogmatic zeal of a priest. This must have been who Bodhidharma was, in the end: a warrior-prince of virtue.

Bodhidharma's practices influenced and transformed the previously existing martial arts of China, creating the famous arts of Shaolin kung fu in the process, with all their many offshoots and derivations.

We apologize to the reader for our long-windedness, but it is essential that each link in the chain of logic and history we have forged be understood, if we are to follow existing historical documents and archaeological findings. And we must acknowledge that, even though each of the aforementioned chain's links is independently verifiable (or at the very least may be independently rigorously examined), the entire chain itself is, admittedly, nothing more than a suggestion.

It is pleasant to speculate, however, that it might indeed be historical truth.

# BIBLIOGRAPHY

Berettas, Marios H. *India Ton Hellenon* [India of the Greeks]. Athens: Georgiades Press, 1996.

Alter, Joseph S. *The Wrestler's Body: Identity and Ideology in North India.* Berkeley: University of California Press, 1992.

Benson, H., J. Lehman et al. "Body Temperature Changes during the Practice of gTummo Yoga." *Nature* 295 (1982): 234–36.

Benson, H., M. S. Malhotra et al. "Three Case Reports of the Metabolic and Electroencephalographic Changes During Advanced Buddhist Meditation Techniques." *Behavioral Medicine* 16, no. 2 (1982): 290–95.

Boardman, John. *Persia and the West.* London: Thames and Hudson, 2000.

Burton, Sir Richard F. *The Book of the Sword.* London: Chatto and Windus, 1884.

Byam, Michele. *Arms & Armour.* Eyewitness Guides. London: Dorling Kindersley, 1989.

Campbell, Joseph. *The Way of the Animal Powers: Mythologies of the Great Hunt.* New York: Harper and Row, 1988.

Council of Europe. "The Roots of Odysseus" in *Gods and Heroes of Bronze Age Europe* [a museum exhibition catalog]. Bonn: Hatje/Conte, Ostfildern-Ruit, 1999, 103–105.

Electronic Journals of Martial Arts and Sciences: http:/www.ejmas.com.

Funakoshi, Gichin. *Karate-Do Kyohan.* Tokyo: Kodansha, 1973.

Haedeke, Hanns-Ulrich. *Blankwaffen.* Solingen: Deutsches Klingenmuseum Solingen, 1982.

Newberry, P. E. *Beni Hasan*. Vol. 1 and 2. London: 1893.

Penrose, Sir Roger, with Abner Shimony, Nancy Cartwright, and Stephen Hawking. *The Large, the Small, and the Human Mind*. London: Cambridge University Press, 2000.

Poliakoff, Michael. *Combat Sports in the Ancient World*. New Haven: Yale University Press, 1987.

Time-Life Books. *The Enterprise of War*. Amsterdam: Time-Life Books, 1991.

Venkatesh, S., et al. "A study of structure of phenomenology of consciousness in meditative and non-meditative states." *Indian Journal of Physiology and Pharmacology* 41, no. 2 (1997): 149–53.

Warry, John. *Warfare in the Classical World*. New York: St. Martin's Press, 1980.

Wheeler, John Archibald, with Kenneth Ford. *Geons, Black Holes and Quantum Foam: A Life in Physics*. New York: W. W. Norton and Company, 1998.

Zabinski, Grzegorz, and Bartlomiej Walczak. *Codex Wallerstein: A Medieval Fighting Book from the Fifteenth Century on the Longsword, Falchion, Dagger, and Wrestling*. Boulder, Colorado: Paladin Press, 2001.

# INDEX

Page numbers in *italic* represent figures.

# BOOKS OF RELATED INTEREST

**Nei Kung**
The Secret Teachings of the Warrior Sages
*by Kosta Danaos*

**The Magus of Java**
Teachings of an Authentic Taoist Immortal
*by Kosta Danaos*

**Chi Kung**
The Chinese Art of Mastering Energy
*by Yves Réquéna*

**Martial Arts Teaching Tales of Power and Paradox**
Freeing the Mind, Focusing Chi,
and Mastering the Self
*by Pascal Fauliot*

**The Spiritual Practices of the Ninja**
Mastering the Four Gates to Freedom
*by Ross Heaven*

**The Spiritual Foundations of Aikido**
*by William Gleason*

**The Warrior Is Silent**
Martial Arts and the Spiritual Path
*by Scott Shaw, Ph.D.*

**The Peaceful Way**
A Children's Guide to the Traditions of
the Martial Arts
*by Claudio Iedwab and Roxanne Standefer*

Inner Traditions • Bear & Company
P.O. Box 388
Rochester, VT 05767
1-800-246-8648
www.InnerTraditions.com

Or contact your local bookseller